instant EXPERT

COLLECTING SPORTS MEMORABILIA

MICHAEL McKEEVER

Alliance Publishers

ISBN 0-9641509-9-9

Cover and interior design by Cynthia Dunne
Produced by Publisher's Studio, Albany, New York

Alliance Books are
available at special discounts for bulk purchases
for sales and promotions, premiums, fund
raising, or educational use.
For details contact:
Alliance Publishing Inc.
P.O. Box 080377
Brooklyn, New York 11208-0002

Distributed to the trade by National Book Network, Inc.

10 8 6 4 2 1 3 5 7 9

ACKNOWLEDGMENTS

This book would not have been possible without the contributions of dozens of people. Their expertise in the areas of evaluations and grading, authentification, preservation, research, and technical support has greatly enhanced this edition. We sincerely appreciate their efforts and want to thank them for their time, dedication, and hard work. They are:

Marty Appel, The Topps Company, Inc.; Bill Barron, NFL Properties; Tim Boyle; Rich Bradley, The Upper Deck Company; Joie Casey, Field of Dreams; Ken Cicola, Vivid Graphics; Lou Costanza, Champion Sports; Mike Cramer, Pacific Trading Cards; Dick DeCourcy, Georgia Music and Sports; Doug Drotman, National Media Group; Joe Esposito, B&E Collectibles; Larry Fritsch, Larry Fritsch Cards; Richard Galasso, Home Plate Collectibles; Steve Galletta, Touchdown Cards; Tony Galovich, American Card Exchange; Richard Gelman, Card Collectors Company; Dick Gilkeson; Bill Goepner, San Diego Sports Collectibles; David Greenhill, New York Card Company; Wayne Grove, First Base Sports Nostalgia; Bill Goodwin, St. Louis Baseball Cards; Walter Hall, Hall's Nostalgia; Eric Handler, Lapin Public Relations; Don Harrison, The Tenth Inning; Bill Henderson (King of the Commons); Neil Hoppenworth; Bob Ibach, Golan/Harris; Donn Jennings, Donn Jennings Cards; Bill Karaman; Martin Kelly, The SportsCard Report Radio show; Bill Kennedy, No Gum Just Cards; Rick Kohl, The Strike Zone; David Kohler, SportsCards Plus; Don LePore; Allen Lewis, Collectors Edge; Lew Lipset; Kay Longmire, O-Pee-Chee of Canada; Greg Manning, Greg Manning Cards; Jim

Mayfield; Terry Melia, *Encyclopedia of Sports Memorabilia;* Blake Meyer, Lone Star Sports Cards; Mike Miller; Dick Millerd; Frank and Steve Pemper, Ball Four Cards; Jack and Patti Petruzzelli, 59 Innings; Warren Power; Andy Rapoza; Peter Reeves (our computer guru); Gavin Riley; Steve Rotman, Rotman Productions; Murray Rubenfield, The SportsCard Report Radio Show; Robert Rusnak; Steve Ryan, *Trading Cards Magazine;* Kevin Savage, The Sports Gallery; Michelle Serrio, The SportsCard Report Radio Show; Ira H. Silverman, Silverman, Warren/Kremer, Inc.; Eric Slutsky, Edelman Public Relations Worldwide; Nigel Spill, Oldies and Goodies; Jim Stevens; Ted Taylor, Fleer Corporation; Joe Valle, Cardboard Dreams; Tom Wall; Bill Wesslund, Portland SportsCards; Chris Widmaier, Silverman, Warren/Kremer, Inc.; Matt Wozniak; and Kit Young, Kit Young Cards.

We especially want to thank Dorothy Harris and the staff at Alliance Publishing.

Photos Courtesy of Trading Cards Magazine

CONTENTS

Introduction

Prized sports memorabilia has never been more popular. From vintage artifacts like a rare Lou Gehrig game-worn jersey to an autographed photo of one of today's hot young phenoms, securing a genuine piece of sports history has, at one time or another, captured the hearts and minds of nearly every sports fan in America.

The growing field of sports memorabilia encompasses a lot of territory. It includes a signed scorecard from a memorable game, an original lithograph of one of the great moments in sports, a ticket stub to a Super Bowl game, or a figurine of your favorite player. All of these items fall under the category of sports collectibles. All evoke memories of a favorite player or a treasured moment in sports history. Some are more valuable than others and some have no value at all except for nostalgia.

Exactly what constitutes sports memorabilia? Where do you find it? How much is it worth? How can you tell if it is real or fake? And how do you preserve those treasured mementos? This is the type of question I've addressed in this book. I've also included a resource page with mailing addresses for all major sports franchises and a glossary to help you understand the hobby terminology.

Over the past decade, collecting sports memorabilia has grown from a cottage industry to a $4 billion-per-year business. An estimated 20 million people actively participate in America's number one hobby. Whether you are a seasoned collector or a beginner, I think you will find the following pages educational, informative, and entertaining. I sincerely hope this book will enhance your enjoyment of the hobby and serve as your official reference guide to the exciting world of sports memorabilia.

CHAPTER 1

How to Get Started in the Hobby

If you have ever attended a sporting event and brought home the game program, a ticket stub, or a souvenir from a concession stand, you are already a memorabilia collector. Nearly everyone has something stashed away in his or her attic or basement that qualifies as sports memorabilia. For most of us, collecting sports memorabilia is a way to enhance the enjoyment of our favorite sport. The fact that a nostalgic memento may appreciate in value over time is an added bonus.

Some collectors are passionate about their hobby, spending their spare time and income tracking down items to add to their collections. Others are passive collectors who save a few items from their personal sports experiences for sentimental reasons. Still others earn their living buying and selling rare and limited collectibles and are part of a hobby that has grown into a multi-billion dollar business in little over a decade.

If you are just starting out and are interested in becoming more involved in this fun-filled hobby, there are some things you should know

Old felt pennants make nice collectibles

before you begin. What should you collect and where should you look for it? Sports memorabilia can be found almost anywhere. It can be bought and sold over the counter at your neighborhood baseball card shop. Professional dealers display it at local and regional baseball card shows or at national sports memorabilia conventions. Auctions are also a good source for vintage sports memorabilia, although the items open to bids are often quite expensive. But some of the best stuff can be found at garage and yard sales, flea markets, antique shops, and thrift stores.

Most collectors start out by concentrating on items that relate to their favorite sport, whether it be baseball, basketball, football, hockey, horse racing, auto racing, or boxing. Some collectors are

Tickets and ticket stubs from playoff games are rising in value

even more specific, focusing on their favorite team or a few select players from their favorite team. To break it down even further, most collectors will concentrate on certain categories of memorabilia, such as autographs, game-used equipment or uniforms, limited edition artwork, or vintage sports publications.

Once you decide on a particular sport and a kind of memorabilia, you should decide how much money you can afford to devote to your new-found hobby. Do you want to collect for fun or investment purposes? The older items are the most expensive, and depending on their scarcity and historical significance, are often the best investments. Newer items are less expensive and considered to be a more speculative investment. To truly enjoy the hobby, always collect what you like and focus on the sport you like best. Visit a few card shows and memorabilia conventions to get a feel for what specific sports collectibles are available and what prices dealers are asking for them. You should subscribe to one or more hobby publications. They all run articles about sports memorabilia, both new material and vintage material—and be sure to read the advertisements. They will give you a glimpse at what is out there and how much it costs.

Most card stores and hobby shops sell autographed memorabilia

There are tons of sports collectibles on the market today and there are tens of thousands of items waiting to be discovered. The true collector likes the chase as much as the acquisition. Putting together a sports memorabilia collection is not easy. It requires time, diligence, patience, and, at times, hard work. It also requires love. Love of sports, the game, the players, and the memories of games gone by.

CHAPTER 2

COLLECTING AUTOGRAPHS

For sports fans, the most coveted sports collectible in the hobby is a souvenir autographed by their favorite star. An autograph gives the collector a way to identify with his or her idol and it offers them a personal connection to the player and the game he plays. Autograph collecting has flourished for over a hundred years, when baseball stars of the day were sought out for their signatures. Today, of all the sports memorabilia in the hobby, none compares in popularity to the autographed collectible.

Over the years, players have signed everything from scrap paper to restaurant napkins, photographs, old newspapers, game programs, balls, bats, gloves, hats, and all types of sports equipment. Authentic autographs can be found on limited edition artwork, figurines, plaques, articles of clothing, body casts, and some items too bizarre to mention. Autographed items have been bought, sold, traded, preserved, and displayed for generations.

The value of autographed memorabilia (as of most sports collectibles) depends on supply and demand. Demand is influenced by such factors as the player's overall popularity, his greatness, the item that is signed, how it was signed, the condition of the autographed item, its scarcity, and its authenticity.

If you are just starting out, there are a few

Signed baseball photos are among the most popular collectibles

general guidelines you should follow before you begin to buy vintage signed memorabilia or obtain new autographs from today's top players. Should you have the player personalize your item? Are single-signed items a better investment than items that contain multiple signatures? What pen should the player use to sign your item? How can you protect yourself against forgeries? And what is the best way to go about collecting autographs of today's top stars?

If you see an autographed sports memento as a potential investment, you should never have your signed item personalized. While it might be nice to own a ball or photograph signed to Frank, Billy, John, Mike, or Larry, it limits the marketability of

Autographed Joe DiMaggio baseball card, valued at over $500

the item. Though a popular salutation such as "Best Wishes," "Good Luck," or "Sincerely" usually will not affect the value of the autographed item, it is best if the player just signs his name and nothing else.

In most cases, a single-signed collectible, that is a memento that contains just one signature, is generally more valuable than a collectible with multiple signatures. The exceptions would be if every signature on the item were autographs of Hall of Famers or perhaps if all the signatures were from members of a championship team. Otherwise, having a Hall of Famer's signature next to an autograph of a lesser known player will diminish the value of the Hall of Famer's signature.

Autographed baseballs are the most popular collectibles in the hobby

Choosing the correct writing instrument is also imperative to maintaining the long-term condition and thus the value of the autographed item. Sharpie pens are a popular choice for most collectors when the memento is a paper item, such as a photograph, sports card, magazine cover or newspaper article. Hard-tipped ballpoint pens are best for baseballs, gloves, and other flexible surfaces where a Sharpie pen may tend to bleed through the surface or smear.

Getting the player to sign only a certain area of the item is often difficult but very important to the future investment potential of the item. You do not want a player signing his John Hancock over his face in a photograph. Try to get him to sign in one of the corners of the photograph, preferably a corner with a light background where the signature will be highly visible. If you are having a baseball signed, get the player to sign on the sweet spot of the ball. It could increase the value of the signed baseball by as much as 50 percent. The sweet spot is the blank area between the seams opposite the official logo and the league president's signature.

Collecting signed memorabilia from legendary players who are deceased can be an expensive proposition, since these items are only available in the secondary market and are relatively scarce. But getting autographs from today's top stars or even living Hall of Famer's can be an enjoyable pursuit. Autographs can be obtained, with patience, by standing outside a stadium gate as players come and go. Baseball card shows and memorabilia conventions are also excellent places to obtain autographs, although you might have to pay a fee to get the signature of a sports star who is being paid to make a personal appearance at a show. Many retired players will sign autographs through the mail and every current team has a public relations staff that tries to accommodate the autograph requests. Always remember to include a self-addressed stamped return envelope with your request.

When requesting an autograph in person or by mail, never bring or send more than a couple of items to be signed. Many players get suspicious if a collector approaches with dozens of articles, thinking that the autograph seeker might be a dealer who intends merely to resell the items for profit. Always be polite when requesting an autograph; like most people, players respond more favorably to those who are polite. Most players do not like to be interrupted when they are out to dinner in a restaurant or out in public with their families. The best time and place to obtain a player's signature is when he is "at work," where many players feel that signing autographs is part of their job and responsibility. Some players have better dispositions than others and treat autograph seekers accordingly. If a player refuses an autograph request, it is his prerog-

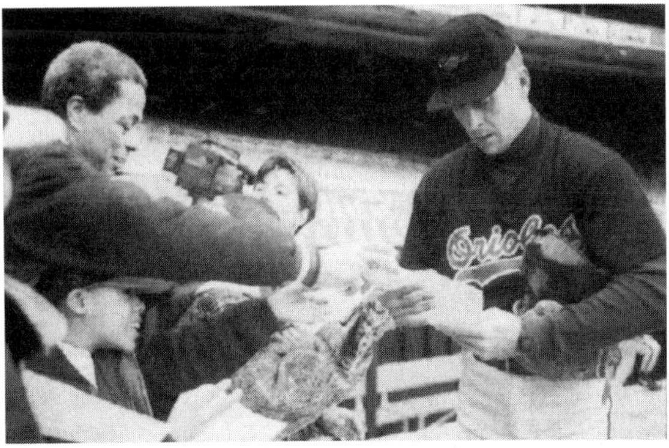

Cal Ripken Jr. graciously signs before an Orioles game

ative and the collector should move on. When sending cards or photographs through the mail to be signed, remember, the player has no obligation to sign it or return it. Never send bulk items such as a ball or a bat to a player through the mail, for these can easily be misplaced or lost.

Beware of Fake Autographs

Unfortunately, the rising value of autographed material has led to an increase in bogus autographs. To protect yourself against these forgeries, learn all you can about this segment of the hobby. If you are buying an autographed item from a dealer, always ask for a receipt. Most reputable dealers will offer one and, in some cases, give you a letter of authenticity. Always ask the dealer where the item came from and from whom he or she bought it. Dealers can be fooled too and may resell bogus items without knowingly trying to cheat their customers.

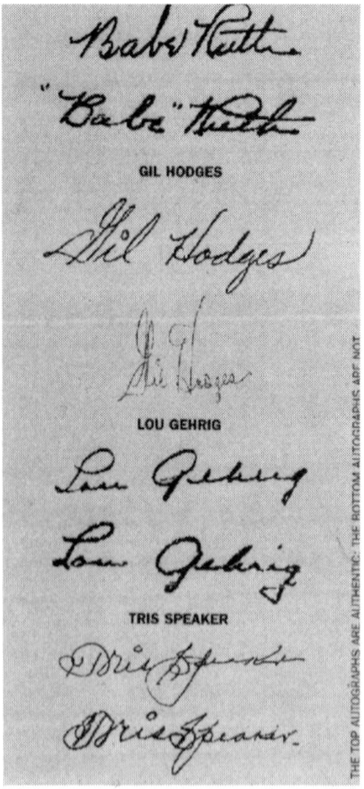

Experts can spot fake autographs by comparing them to real ones

Most dealers will offer a money-back guarantee if the item proves to be a fake. Experts can usually tell if an autographed item is real or not.

For older material, experts can compare signatures to those they know are valid or they can examine the ink used on the signature. A Babe Ruth signature signed with a ballpoint pen is probably a phony because ballpoint pens were introduced in the late 1940s and Ruth died in 1948. Collectors should also do their homework and study a little baseball history. Each official major league baseball comes with a facsimile signature of the president of the league. A Honus Wagner autograph on a baseball that also contains a signature of former National League President Warren Giles would obviously be a fake, since Wagner died long before Giles assumed the title of National League president.

Autographs of current stars are much easier to authenticate by actually comparing them to their true signatures currently in circulation. In all cases, do your homework. Buy from a dealer who has been around a while and will be in business tomorrow. If it is an expensive item, get a second, even third opinion from another dealer or autograph expert.

Letters of Authenticity often accompany memorabilia to verify its validity

Collectors of autographed memorabilia also need to be aware of facsimile autographs and ghost signers. Facsimile autographs are printed or stamped onto an item by a machine and are easy to spot because the signatures on the items in question are exactly the same. A collectible containing a facsimile autograph has no appreciable value. Ghost signing was prevalent in the 1940s, 1950s, and 1960s, long before there was a market for autographed memorabilia. It was not uncommon for ball players back then to turn over the signing chores to a clubhouse attendant or a bat boy. The players, who were often asked to signed baseballs by the dozen, were not out to cheat anyone because their signatures had no market value back then. Today an autograph expert can easily detect a ghost signer's autograph simply by comparing it to an authentic one. The best guarantee of the validity of an autograph is getting it in person where you can witness the player signing. In the case of the more expensive, vintage material, get a second or third opinion before spending your hard-earned dollars on a signed collectible.

CHAPTER 3

AUTOGRAPHED BASEBALL MEMORABILIA

The single-signed baseball is not only the most popular sports collectible in the hobby today, it is also one of the most affordable. The baseball of choice is an official American League or National League baseball or an official World Series or All-Star game baseball as long as the player signing the ball was a member of a par-

Autographed Mickey Mantle baseball, valued at over $125

Authentic Babe Ruth baseball, valued at over $4,500

ticipating team. The highest value is for brand new baseballs, not game-used balls, unless the game-used ball carries some historical significance such as a memorable home run, a no-hitter, or some other documented milestone. The baseball should be signed in ballpoint ink and centered between the seams of the ball, horizontally, on the sweet spot, which is opposite the official logo and league president's signature.

Baseballs with multiple signatures are often worth less than single-signed baseballs, especially when a Hall of Famer's signature appears next to a lesser known player. Exceptions would include a baseball signed by all the members of a championship team or a ball signed by Hall of Famers.

The signatures of Hall of Famers, both living and deceased, are generally worth more than those of today's top stars. Autographs of deceased players usually rise in value because the player is no longer around to sign additional items. An autograph from a former superstar like the late Roberto Clemente is one of the most difficult signatures to acquire. He did not sign many items while he was alive and those he did rarely come on the secondary market. A Clemente single-signed baseball can command

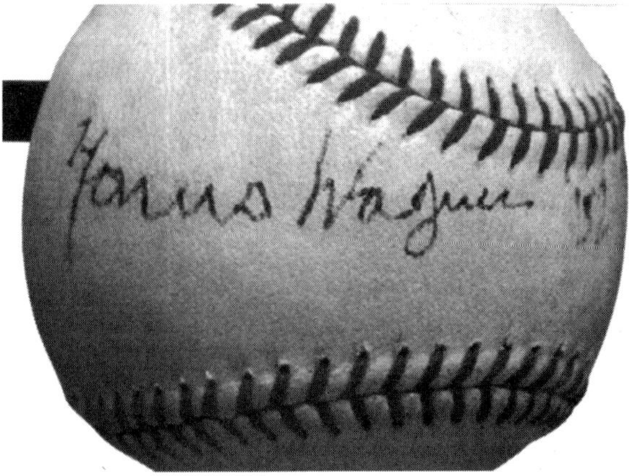

Baseball signed by Honus Wagner, commands over $4,000

up to $2,500. A baseball signed by former Yankees catcher Thurman Munson, killed in a plane crash in 1979, is valued at around $750. Following Mickey Mantle's death, the value of his autographed baseballs jumped from around $90 to $125. A baseball signed by Babe Ruth is worth over $4,500.

While tracking down baseballs of deceased Hall of Famers can be an expensive proposition, obtaining signed baseballs from living Hall of Famers can be inexpensive and easy. Many former greats appear regularly at large baseball card shows and memorabilia conventions. Legends like Hank Aaron, Willie Mays, Eddie Mathews, Ernie Banks, Brooks Robinson, Al Kaline, Yogie Berra, Whitey Ford, and Steve Carlton charge between $10 and $35 to sign an item. Many memorabilia dealers offer signed baseballs from these players for $50 to $75 each. These signed baseballs will not appreciate very fast because most of these players continually sign items and there are thousands of signed baseballs from each player in circulation. Single-signed baseballs from all-time greats like Joe DiMaggio ($150) and Ted Williams ($125) are worth more both because the players are legendary

SINGLE-SIGNED BASEBALLS (LEGENDS)

Lou Gehrig	$5,000
Babe Ruth	4,500
Cy Young	4,500
Honus Wagner	4,000
Nap Lajoie	3,750
Al Simmons	3,500
Jackie Robinson	3,000
Roberto Clemente	2,500
Ty Cobb	2,500
Jimmy Foxx	2,500
Rogers Hornsby	2,500
Mel Ott	2,000
Dizzy Dean	750
Roy Campanella	500
Lefty Grove	375
Roger Maris	175

and because there are relatively few baseballs signed by them in circulation.

If you cannot attend a major baseball card show in person, many show promoters will offer mail-order signings. Of course, you would not get to meet the player in person but at least you could add another famous autograph to your collection. Check some of the hobby publications for advertisements, mailing instructions, and fees.

Collecting autographs from today's top stars is relatively easy. You can hang around the ball parks or a player's hotel. You can also send requests to individual teams who usually assign a member of their public relations staff to try to fulfill your request. In each case it may take time and require patience, but more often than not you will come

SINGLE-SIGNED BASEBALLS (CURRENT)

Sandy Koufax	$80
Reggie Jackson	60
Nolan Ryan	60
Barry Bonds	50
Ken Griffey Jr.	50
Cal Ripken Jr.	50
Mike Schmidt	50
Frank Thomas	50
Carl Yastzremski	50
Hank Aaron	40
Johnny Bench	40
George Brett	40
Roger Clemens	40
Kirby Puckett	40
Ryne Sandberg	40
Ozzie Smith	40
Dave Winfield	40
Robin Yount	40

away with the signature you want. Besides, half the fun of getting the autograph is in the pursuit.

Besides single-signed baseballs, other highly valued collectibles include signed bats, hats, batting helmets, batting gloves, replica jerseys, and photographs. With the exception of signed photos, most of these items are considered bulk items and, if you are lucky enough to own one, players will charge more to sign these collectibles at card shows and memorabilia conventions. Actual game-worn equipment is worth more than replica equipment. (See the chapter on game-used memorabilia.) Replica jerseys, team hats, and batting helmets are among the many items that are officially licensed

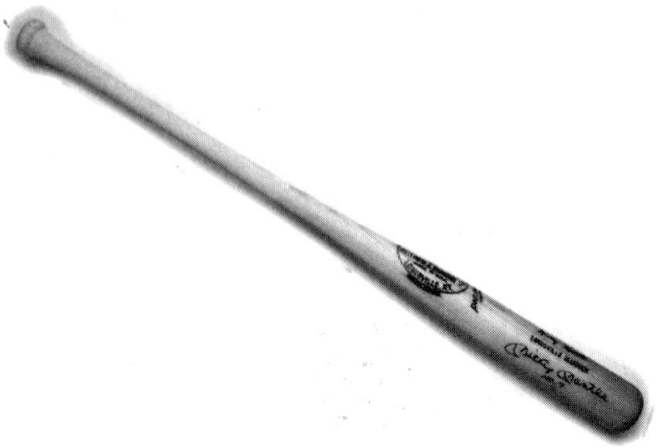

Game-used Mickey Mantle bat, sells for over $10,000

by Major League Baseball and sold unsigned at sporting goods stores, major department stores, and discount chains. Hobbyists will often buy these products and carry them to games or memorabilia shows to obtain a player's signature.

Memorabilia dealers often have autographed material for sale in their shops. If you do not have the time or the patience to track down individual players for their autographs, try a local dealer or read the advertisements in the hobby publications. Many dealers have already done the legwork for you and earn a nice living for their efforts.

Baseball bat used by Babe Ruth, valued at over $25,000

Autographed Football Memorabilia

While baseball has been the driving force in the hobby for over half a century, the rising value of football memorabilia mirrors the increased popularity of the sport over the last two decades. Collectors of football memorabilia have nearly as many options as baseball collectors. From signed footballs to autographed photos to helmets, mini-helmets, and replica jerseys, the possibilities are endless.

As with baseball memorabilia, the vintage items are the most valuable football col-

Football signed by Joe Montana and Dan Marino, valued at $425

Autographed football helmets are hot collectibles

lectibles. Pre-1970 football memorabilia is one of the fastest growing segments of the hobby. A signed official NFL (National Football League) football is the collectible of choice for football hobbyists. Authentic game-worn equipment such as jerseys and helmets are rare and highly valued collectibles. NFL Properties, the licensing arm of the NFL, is very aggressive when it comes to licensing new products, and two products, a white-paneled football suitable for autographs, and NFL mini-helmets, have become increasingly popular with collectors.

Signed Joe Montana football, worth over $250

A brand new, official NFL football should be used when acquiring players' autographs. Official NFL footballs can be bought at most retail sporting goods stores or major department and discount chains. When getting a player's signature, always ask him to sign on the panel opposite the official logo. A thick, hard-tipped pen is still the writing instrument of choice, but a Sharpie pen can also be used, especially if the football will be encased in a plastic or glass ball holder. The newer white-paneled footballs may add a nice visual contrast to the autograph, but a signature on an official NFL football can be worth up to 40 percent more in the long run.

SINGLE-SIGNED FOOTBALLS (LEGENDS)

Jim Thorpe	$6,000
Red Grange	1,000
Vince Lombardi	400
Sammy Baugh	350
Bronko Nagurski	350
Joe Montana	275
Paul Brown	250
George Halas	250
O. J. Simpson	250
Jack Kemp	200
Joe Namath	200
Terry Bradshaw	175
Jim Brown	175
Frank Gifford	175
Otto Graham	175
Walter Payton	175
Roger Staubach	175
Johnny Unitas	175

SINGLE-SIGNED FOOTBALLS (CURRENT)

Emmitt Smith	$250
Barry Sanders	225
Troy Aikman	200
Dan Marino	200
Jerry Rice	200
Steve Young	180
John Elway	175
Marcus Allen	150
Drew Bledsoe	150
Marshall Faulk	150
Brett Favre	150
Michael Irvin	150
Jim Kelly	125
Warren Moon	125
Deion Sanders	125
Thurman Thomas	125

Team-signed footballs make great souvenirs but, as on baseballs, multiple signatures could diminish the overall value of the most expensive autograph on the ball. Single-signed footballs, especially if the player is a Hall of Famer, will be worth more in the long run, unless the multiple-signed football is from a Super Bowl championship team and all the members of the team signed the football.

One of the most popular new collectibles in the hobby is the NFL mini-helmet. These are smaller versions of each team's official NFL helmet and are ideal for obtaining signatures. The mini-helmets are easy to carry to memorabilia shows or stadiums and easy to display. Many dealers of sports paraphernalia report mini-helmets to be among the fastest growing items in their inventory. And many

Official NFL team helmets are rising in value

dealers of sports memorabilia have already tracked down players and offer signed versions of the mini-helmets for sale in their shops.

The demand for autographed football memorabilia does not come close to matching the demand for signed baseball items. By comparison, many football collectibles are considered bargains in today's hobby. While dozens of baseball collectibles have been sold by auction at six-figure prices, no football memorabilia has come close. For this reason, many experts feel football memorabilia has more long-term growth potential than baseball.

CHAPTER 5

AUTOGRAPHED BASKETBALL MEMORABILIA

The spectacular evolution of basketball over the past fifteen years has been one of the biggest stories in sports. As recently as the mid-1980s, no major trading card company was producing basketball cards, and interest in the sport had been waning. The emergence of Larry Bird and Magic Johnson in the early '80s and Michael Jordan in the late '80s changed all that. Basketball has become the fastest growing

Basketball signed by Larry Bird and Magic Johnson, valued at over $500

spectator sport in America and with its rising popularity, collectors have turned their attention to the memorabilia of some of the game's biggest stars.

Today, Michael Jordan has emerged as the hobby's biggest star, a position that had been occupied for generations by baseball's Hall of Famers. A signed souvenir from Jordan is the most sought-after collectible in the hobby. The renewed popularity of the game even has some collectors rediscovering the legends from the past and today their collectibles are experiencing a rebirth. Autographs of such greats as Bill Russell, Bob Cousy,

SINGLE-SIGNED BASKETBALLS (LEGENDS)

Bill Russell	$600
Wilt Chamberlain	375
Larry Bird	300
Magic Johnson	300
Julius Erving	275
Bill Bradley	200
Phil Jackson	200
Willis Reed	200
Oscar Robertson	200
Jerry West	200
Lenny Wilkins	200
Red Auerbach	175
Kareem Abdul Jabbar	175
Bob Cousey	175
Pete Maravich	175
George Mikan	175
Elgin Baylor	150
Walt Frazier	150
John Havlicek	150

Wilt Chamberlain, Jerry West, Oscar Robertson, and Julius Erving are in high demand. Russell's are especially valuable, since he refused to sign autographs for nearly thirty years until he signed a limited number of items at a memorabilia show in 1994. The sudden interest in old basketball memorabilia can be attributed to the scarcity of those items, the new popularity of the game, and the impact that Michael Jordan has had on the memorabilia market.

For hoop fans and collectors, single-signed basketballs are the items to be treasured the most.

The rising popularity of the NBA has created a huge demand for basketball memorabilia

Autographed Jerry West basketball, valued at $150

Game-used equipment, from jerseys to sneakers, are also highly valued but extremely rare collectibles. The demand for signed photos, posters, plaques, replica jerseys, and limited original artwork has shot up.

The basketball of choice is an official NBA (National Basketball Association) basketball, which can be purchased at most major sporting goods, discount and department stores. Since the surface of the basketball is not smooth, a thick, hard-tipped pen or a Sharpie pen is the writing instrument of choice. Always try to get the player to sign the basketball on the panel just above the brand name and logo. That way, for display purposes, both the signature and the official logo will be visible. Team-signed basketballs make nice collectibles but, as on baseballs and footballs, multiple signatures on a basketball could diminish the overall value of the autograph of the team's biggest star. For instance, a basketball signed by all the members of the 1981–82 Boston Celtics is worth about the same as a single-signed basketball by Larry Bird, and the

A pair of game-worn basketball sneakers, among the rarest collectibles in the hobby

basketball with the solitary Bird signature will appreciate faster than the team-signed ball. Exceptions would be basketballs signed by all the members of a championship team. A ball signed by the members of the 1979–80 Los Angeles Lakers is valued in the $1,500 range. A basketball containing all the signatures from the 1992 U.S. Olympic Team, the Dream Team, is worth close to $2,000.

Since basketball is a relatively new sport, rising to prominence in the second half of the 20th century, many of the game's all-time greats are still living, making the challenge to secure an autograph a little easier than with vintage baseball and football memorabilia. However, many memorabilia show promoters say that legendary basketball players tend to be more reclusive than their counterparts in other sports and you rarely see them signing at card shows and conventions. It may require a bit more detective work to gain their autographs, but hobby dealers who buy and sell signed memorabilia often will come across authentic basketball items that they will sell in their shops or through the mail. Check out the advertisements in hobby publications for signed basketball memorabilia.

SINGLE-SIGNED BASKETBALLS (CURRENT)

Michael Jordan	$375
Shaquille O'Neal	250
Hakeem Olajuwon	200
David Robinson	200
Charles Barkley	175
Clyde Drexler	150
Patrick Ewing	150
Anfernee Hardaway	150
Grant Hill	150
Karl Malone	150
Alonzo Mourning	150
John Stockton	150
Dominique Wilkins	150
Larry Johnson	125
Shawn Kemp	125
Jason Kidd	125
Glenn Robinson	125
Chris Webber	125

AUTOGRAPHED HOCKEY MEMORABILIA

While basketball is a relative newcomer on the modern sports scene, hockey is nearly as old as baseball, with vintage artifacts dating all the way back to just after the turn of the century. And because of its scarcity, some vintage hockey memorabilia is just as valuable as the rarest baseball collectibles. For the first half of the century, hockey, a national passion in Canada, was primarily a regional sport in America. Canada had professional leagues, junior leagues, and amateur leagues of all types. In America, major league professional hockey was confined to teams in New York, Boston, Chicago, and Detroit. Professional ice hockey, like baseball, has a storied history, with legendary figures whose feats in the rink have been well-chronicled by those who followed the game.

Over the past twenty-five years, professional ice hockey has emerged as a major sport with a national following in all areas of the United States. The expansion of the National Hockey League in the South and West and promotions of trading card manufacturers and memorabilia dealers have all contributed to hockey's increased popularity. Today, interest in hockey

Hockey puck signed by Gordie Howe, worth $25

memorabilia has never been higher. Vintage memorabilia from some of the game's all-time greats is so scarce in America that prices have surged to record-breaking levels in recent years. Collectors of hockey memorabilia have created a huge demand for autographed items such as hockey pucks, game-used sticks and jerseys, replica jerseys, signed photographs, posters, sports cards, limited edition lithographs, and other original artworks.

The single-signed hockey puck is the most popular collectible in the hockey segment of the hobby. Official hockey pucks can be bought in most major sporting goods and department stores. Many mem-

Game-used Wayne Gretzky jersey, can command up to $20,000 in secondary market

orabilia dealers who sell autographed memorabilia have some signed hockey pucks for sale in their shops, particularly in the Northeast and Midwest. Hockey collectors who live in the sunbelt states where hockey memorabilia is still rather scarce can order signed items by mail from dealers specializing in hockey memorabilia. Check the advertisements in the hobby publications. Regional and national memorabilia conventions are also a good source of signed hockey collectibles.

If you are bringing your own hockey puck to a game or a memorabilia show to try to obtain a player's signature, always bring along a pen with white ink since the hockey puck has a dark surface. It is always best to have the player sign on the black rather than within a logo. Officially licensed NHL merchandise includes hockey pucks with the NHL logo, individual team logos, and special event logos such as an All-Star game logo. Any of these pucks should serve the purpose nicely; more valuable would be a game-used puck with some historical significance.

SINGLE-SIGNED HOCKEY PUCKS (LEGENDS)

Doug Harvey	$300	Turk Broda	$45
Tim Horton	300	Phil Esposito	45
Terry Sawchuk	300	Gordie Howe	45
Jacque Plante	200	Bobby Hull	45
Ken Dryden	125	Maurice Richard	40
Syl Apps, Sr.	90	Guy LaFleur	35
Bobby Orr	80	Bobby Clarke	25
Woody Dumart	75	Tony Esposito	25

Autographed Gordie Howe jersey, valued at $15,000 to $20,000

SINGLE-SIGNED HOCKEY PUCKS (CURRENT)

Wayne Gretzky	75	Pavel Bure	30
Mario Lemieux	50	Paul Coffey	30
Eric Lindros	50	Ed Belfour	25
Sergei Fedorov	40	Nicklas Lidstrom	25
Patrick Roy	40	Alexander Mogilny	25
Brett Hull	35	Jeremy Roenick	25
Jaromir Jagr	35	Teemu Selanne	25
Mark Messier	35	Steve Yzerman	25
Martin Brodeur	30		

COLLECTING GAME-USED EQUIPMENT

CHAPTER 7

If autographed memorabilia is the most popular collectible in the hobby, game-used equipment is easily the most valuable. The scarcity of game-worn baseball, football, basketball, and hockey jerseys, game-used bats, hockey sticks, baseball and football helmets, gloves,

Actual game-worn baseball jerseys are among the most valuable collectibles in the hobby

Several hobby dealers specialize in game-worn uniforms

GAME-WORN BASEBALL UNIFORMS (ALL-TIME)

1927	Lou Gehrig Yankees jersey	$363,000
1938	Lou Gehrig Yankees road jersey	225,000
1942	Jimmie Foxx Red Sox home jersey	220,000
1937	Lou Gehrig Yankees jersey	198,000
1924	Ty Cobb Tigers uniform	176,000
1938	Babe Ruth Coaches jersey (Dodgers)	175,000
1954	Mickey Mantle Yankees jersey	165,000
1968	Nolan Ryan Mets jersey	137,000
1929	Babe Ruth Yankees jersey	132,000
1961	Roger Maris Yankees jersey	132,000
1938	Joe DiMaggio Yankees jersey	132,000
1942	Mel Ott Giants home jersey	121,000

spikes, and sneakers makes them some of the most sought-after collectibles in the world. Vintage material, pre-1970, is so rare and valuable it is usually only available at auctions, with bids boosting the price of an item to record levels nearly every time the collectible is resold.

As does all other sports memorabilia, game-used equipment derives its value by supply and demand, the player's status, the condition of the item, and its authenticity. Uniforms once worn by Hall of Famers, award winners, or record setters are the hottest commodity in this area of the hobby, with old baseball jerseys being at the top of the list.

A New York Yankees jersey worn by Lou Gehrig in 1927 sold for a record $363,000 at an auction in San Francisco in 1993. Today, authentic uniforms once worn by such Hall of Famers as Hank Aaron, Sandy Koufax, Ernie Banks, and Brooks Robinson command up to $20,000 in the secondary market. Recent inductees into the Hall of Fame, such as Mike Schmidt and Reggie Jack-

GAME-WORN BASEBALL JERSEYS (CURRENT)

Ken Griffey Jr.	$3,000
Frank Thomas	3,000
Barry Bonds	2,800
Cal Ripken Jr.	2,800
Kirby Puckett	2,000
Roger Clemens	2,000
Tony Gwynn	2,000
Paul Molitor	2,000
Don Mattingly	1,500
Ozzie Smith	1,500
Mike Piazza	1,250

1960
Ted Williams
Red Sox jersey.

son, have seen their game-worn jerseys sell for as much as $5,000. Future inductees like Nolan Ryan ($5,000), George Brett, Robin Yount, and Dave Winfield ($2,500) all have game-worn jerseys in circulation that command big bucks.

Game-worn jerseys of football greats like Sammy Baugh and Otto Graham sell for as much as $10,000 each; an authentic Joe Montana 49ers jersey will set you back $4,500. Dallas Cowboys stars

Game-used Joe Namath jersey, worth up to $6,000

Emmitt Smith and Troy Aikman have jerseys valued in the $2,500 range. Game-worn basketball jerseys of Larry Bird or Magic Johnson range from $4,000 to $6,000, while a game-worn Wayne Gretzky jersey has sold for as much as $20,000.

Because the value of game-worn jerseys has risen to astronomical levels, many collectors are turning to more affordable replica jerseys, which are manufactured to look and feel exactly like the originals. Replica jerseys sell in the $100 to $200 range and many hobby dealers offer autographed versions for $200 to $300. Some replica jerseys look so real they have been passed off as authentic game-worn versions by unethical dealers.

GAME-WORN FOOTBALL JERSEYS (ALL-TIME)

Jim Thorpe	$50,000
Bronko Nagurski	40,000
Red Grange	35,000
Sammy Baugh	10,000
Otto Graham	10,000
Tom Landry (Giants)	8,000
Jim Brown	6,500
Bobby Layne	6,000
Joe Namath	6,000
Frank Gifford	5,000
Joe Montana	4,800
Gale Sayers	4,000
Paul Hornung	3,500
Johnny Unitas	3,000
Walter Payton	2,800
Roger Staubach	2,800

GAME-WORN FOOTBALL JERSEYS (CURRENT)

Emmitt Smith	$2,800
Dan Marino	2,600
Jerry Rice	2,600
Troy Aikman	2,500
Barry Sanders	2,500
Steve Young	2,400
John Elway	2,000
Drew Bledsoe	1,500
Jim Kelly	1,500
Warren Moon	1,500
Michael Irvin	1,400
Deion Sanders	1,400
Marcus Allen	1,250
Marshall Faulk	1,250

To keep from being defrauded, collectors of game-worn equipment should study the history of their favorite sport to familiarize themselves with the types of uniforms available in each era. Baseball uniforms have been manufactured for more than 125 years by such companies as Spaulding, Rawlings, Wilson, Goodman, MacGregor, MacAuliffe, SandKnit, and Russell. Prior to 1970, uniforms were made of wool flannel or a combination of wool and cotton. Since the early 1970s, manufacturers have produced modern uniforms made out of double knits and polyester.

Unlike most memorabilia that places a premium on mint condition, game-worn jerseys should show some obvious wear. Frayed collars, faded lettering, and fabric softened by hundreds of washings are just a few of the signs to look for to determine if a uniform was actually worn in a game. Always check the manufacturer's tag on the inside of the shirt and try to verify it by calling the team and asking which brand it was using that year. Experts go so far as to check the actual stitching on a uniform by comparing it to a uniform from the same team and the same season.

Another factor in the value of a game-worn jersey is whether it is a home or road jersey. Also, a uniform with the player's name and number on the back will usually command a premium price. However, numbers did not appear on uniforms until the New York Yankees introduced the concept on their road uniforms in 1929. Knowing a little history of the sport could alert you to the fact that, for instance, a 1927 Yankees uniform with a number stitched on the back is a fake. Uniforms from defunct teams such as the Brooklyn Dodgers, Boston Braves, and St. Louis Browns are extremely scarce and usually command top dollar on the secondary market.

Game-used baseball bats, gloves, and batting helmets are also highly valued artifacts, especially if they have been signed by the player. A game-used Babe Ruth bat is worth around $25,000. Game-used bats signed by Lou Gehrig or Ty Cobb are valued in the $20,000 range, by Joe DiMaggio or Mickey Mantle $10,000, by Hank Aaron or Carl Yastrzem-

Autographed batting helmets are considered rare and valuable

Basketball jerseys on display in memorabilia shop

GAME-WORN BASKETBALL JERSEYS (LEGENDS)

Bill Russell	$15,000
Wilt Chamberlain	12,500
Bob Cousy	12,000
George Mikan	10,000
Julius Erving	6,000
Elgin Baylor	5,000
Larry Bird	5,000
Magic Johnson	5,000
Pete Maravich	5,000
Oscar Robertson	5,000
Jerry West	5,000
John Havlicek	4,500
Earl Monroe	4,000
Kareem Abdul Jabbar	3,800
Walt Frazier	3,500

ski $3,000 to $4,000. Among today's top stars, game-used bats signed by Ken Griffey Jr. or Frank Thomas are valued in the $600 to $700 range.

Authentic game-worn football helmets are also highly valued collectibles with prices ranging from $250 for a common player to several thousand dollars for a superstar's helmet. A game-used Joe Montana 49ers helmet recently sold for around $5,000. Signed hockey sticks are another hot item with values ranging from $50 for a common player up to $2,500 for sticks used and signed by Gordie Howe, Bobby Orr, or Maurice Richard. Game-worn basketball sneakers are among the most unique collectibles in the hobby. A pair of basketball sneakers once worn by Hall of Famer Julius Erving recently sold for $1,500 at a charity auction.

GAME-WORN BASKETBALL JERSEYS (CURRENT)

Michael Jordan	$7,000
Shaquille O'Neal	3,500
Hakeem Olajuwon	3,500
Charles Barkley	3,200
Patrick Ewing	3,000
David Robinson	3,000
Anfernee Hardaway	1,600
Clyde Drexler	1,500
Grant Hill	1,250
Karl Malone	1,250
John Stockton	1,250
Alonzo Mourning	1,200
Dominique Wilkins	1,200
Jamal Mashburn	1,200
Reggie Miller	1,100
Shawn Kemp	1,000

Although it is nearly impossible for the average collector to put in the time and diligence required to track down authentic game-worn collectibles, many hobby dealers make their living buying and selling these rare and valuable relics. When buying an authentic game-used item, whether at an auction or from a dealer, you should know the reputation of the seller and get a money-back guarantee in case the item proves to be bogus. Most reputable hobby dealers have a return policy.

GAME-WORN HOCKEY JERSEYS (LEGENDS)

Gordie How	$20,000
Bobby Orr	15,000
Maurice Richard	15,000
Eddie Shore	14,000
Bobby Hull	12,500
Jean Beliveau	11,000
Woody Dumart	10,000
Phil Esposito	10,000
Emile Francis	10,000
Jacque Plante	10,000
Terry Sawchuk	10,000
Doug Harvey	8,500
Sid Abel	8,000
Syl Apps Sr.	8,000
Boom Boom Geoffrion	7,500
Tom Johnson	7,500
Ken Dryden	6,000
Frank Mahovlich	6,000
Guy Lefleur	5,000
Stan Mikita	5,000

This Gordie Howe jersey sold for $18,500 at an auction

GAME-WORN HOCKEY JERSEYS (CURRENT)

Wayne Gretzky	$20,000
Mark Messier	7,500
Mario Lemieux	7,000
Eric Lindros	4,500
Paul Coffey	4,000
Sergei Fedorov	4,000
Brett Hull	4,000
Patrick Roy	4,000
Grant Fuhr	3,000
Teemu Selanne	3,000
Jarmir Jagr	2,800
Alexander Mogilny	2,500
Luc Robitaille	2,200
Jari Kurri	2,000
Steve Yzerman	1,800
Doug Gilmour	1,500

CHAPTER 8

Buttons, Pins, and Rings

Although they are some of the smallest collectibles in sports memorabilia, buttons, pins, and rings are among the rarest and most valuable collectibles in the hobby. Baseball buttons and pins are nearly as old as the game itself. As were early baseball cards, many of the vintage buttons and pins were issued as premiums by cigarette and candy companies. Sweet Caporal cigarettes produced baseball pins from 1910 to 1912 and so far around 150 pins from that set have been discovered. The most valuable pin from this group is the Ty Cobb pin, worth around $250 to $300 in near-mint condition.

Over the last eighty years, millions of buttons and pins have been issued with such products as candy, cereals, colas, cookies, hot dogs, ice cream, milk, and potato chips. Nearly every sport has had pins produced as premiums or used as give-away promotions from baseball, football, basketball, and hockey, to the Olympic Games, boxing, auto racing, horse racing, golf, and bowling. With rare exceptions, the value for most of these pins would range between 50 cents to $100 depending on the pin's age, subject, scarcity, and condition.

Old press pins and championship rings are extremely difficult to find

In 1956, Topps issued a set of sixty baseball pins which sells for around $3,000 today in near-mint condition. Individual pins of Hall of Famers from that set command up to $100 each. Collectors interested in buying, selling, or trading collectible pins can be found at most major regional baseball card shows and memorabilia conventions. Some memorabilia dealers specialize in pins and often have huge displays at these hobby events. The popularity of sports-related collectible pins has risen steadily over the past ten years and many of today's top sports card and memorabilia companies have reintroduced the tiny collectible as part of their growing inventory of new products.

Press Pins

Among the most coveted and valuable collectibles in the hobby are press pins, which are given to the working media who cover such major events as the World Series, All-Star Games, Super Bowls, and major college football bowl games. Since these rare collectibles memorialize a historical sporting event and because production is extremely limited, these pins have become some of the most expensive mementos in the hobby.

The first World Series press pin was introduced by the Philadelphia A's for the 1911 World Series. Like many early press pins, it came with a ribbon

MOST VALUABLE PRESS PINS (BASEBALL)

1911	Philadelphia A's	$15,000
1919	Chicago White Sox	12,500
1912	New York Giants	8,500
1938	Cincinnati (All-Star)	7,500
1914	Philadelphia A's	7,250
1915	Philadelphia Phillies	7,000
1913	New York Giants	6,500
1913	Philadelphia A's	6,000
1917	Chicago White Sox	5,500
1917	New York Giants	4,500
1915	Boston Red Sox	4,000
1930	Philadelphia A's	3,500
1935	Chicago Cubs	3,000
1943	St. Louis Cardinals	2,600
1956	Brooklyn Dodgers	2,500
1941	Detroit Tigers (All-Star)	2,400
1948	St. Louis Cardinals (All-Star)	2,000

attached. Today that pin, with the ribbon intact and in good condition, is valued at over $15,000. Unfortunately, most early press pins have been found without the ribbon, which diminishes the value of the pin by 75 percent. All press pins issued from 1911 through World War II are considered extremely rare and command top dollar.

Over the past forty years, teams started producing press pins in larger quantities to accommodate the growing number of media covering each championship or All-Star event. Today those press pins are fairly easy to locate and are reasonably priced, usually in the $50 to $400 range.

In baseball, the American League and National League champions are responsible for producing

MOST VALUABLE PRESS PINS (FOOTBALL)

Super Bowl I	$1,600
Super Bowl II	1,300
Super Bowl III	1,000
Super Bowl VI	500
Super Bowl VII	400
Super Bowl VIII	375
Super Bowl X	350
Super Bowl IX	300
Super Bowl XII	300
Super Bowl XI	250

and distributing World Series press pins. The host team for the annual All-Star game is responsible for those press pins. Since pennant races often go down to the wire in any given season, more than one team in each league sometimes places an order for World Series press pins. The pins from teams that did not make it to the World Series are called phantom press pins in the hobby. Occasionally, these phanton pins make their way into circulation and some can be quite valuable. A phantom pin made for the 1950 Brooklyn Dodgers is valued at $2,500, while the press pin from the actual pennant winner that year, the 1950 Philadelphia Phillies, goes for around $275. There is a market for phanton press pins as long as the pins are dated and cannot be used again. However, some teams have placed advance orders for World Series press pins without dates. If they fail to make it to the World Series that year, they can use the pins in the future. The demand is small for these pins and they have little value.

CHAMPIONSHIP RINGS

For any athlete, professional or amateur, winning a championship is the ultimate goal. In most cases, players who are part of a championship team are awarded rings to commemorate the accomplishment. It is not uncommon for some of these rings to find their way into the sports memorabilia market. Until twenty-five years ago it was generally believed that these rare and precious mementos found their way into the market when a former player, perhaps down on his luck, was forced to pawn his championship ring. That may have been the case in the past, but today it is not uncommon for teams to order hundreds of championship rings to distribute, not just to the players, but to front office staff, scouts, medical staff, grounds crew, and even broadcasting staff.

While World Series rings, Super Bowl rings, and All-Star rings are the most valuable, rings are often awarded to league champions, winners of major college football bowl games, and champions in many individual sports, such as boxing, tennis,

Sample of Dallas Cowboys championship ring, worth over $10,000

and golf. Limited edition rings have also been produced to honor special milestones in an athlete's career and are considered valuable collectibles.

No matter how rings enter the secondary memorabilia market, there is a strong demand for them. Some of the rings that have been in circulation include a Washington Redskins Super Bowl XXII ring valued at over $15,000, a 1990 New York Giants Super Bowl ring ($4,000), a 1969 New York Jets 10k gold Super Bowl III ring ($3,200), a 1971 Dallas Cowboys 10k gold Super Bowl VI ring ($3,200), a 1969 New York Mets 10k gold World Series ring ($2,200), a 1980 Oakland Raiders Super Bowl ring ($3,500), a 1990 Detroit Pistons NBA championship ring ($2,650), a 1991 Pittsburgh Penguins Stanley Cup championship ring ($3,500), a 1976 Montreal Canadians Stanley Cup Championship ring ($1,650), and a 1960 New York Yankees American League Championship ring ($4,250).

The value of individual rings depends not only on scarcity but also on design. Some teams are more extravagant than others when it comes to ring design and include lots of gold, diamonds, and other jewels. Also, many of the championship rings in circulation today are sales samples which manufacturers use to demonstrate various designs and styles.

Green Bay Packers championship ring, commands over $12,000 in the secondary market

When sales samples find their way into the secondary memorabilia market, they are labeled with an "(SS)". When sales samples mirror the design of a team's actual ring, they can be just as valuable as the actual championship ring. However, many sales samples contain cubic zirconium rather than real diamonds; collectors who buy sales samples often add diamonds to the rings after their purchase.

The company that makes many of the championship rings, Balfour, also produces limited edition copies of rings that mark special events for Hall of Fame inductions or retirement ceremonies for legendary superstars. Many of these limited edition rings can range from as few as ten to as many as 200. These rings usually feature 10k gold with a diamond or diamond clusters and sell for thousands of dollars.

Several hobby dealers throughout the country specialize in locating and reselling rings. The Ring Man in Philadelphia always seems to have a large inventory of these championship mementos for sale. Out of This World Memorabilia in San Pedro, California, also specializes in rare sports rings. Collectors can expect to pay from $450 for a college bowl game championship ring to $20,000 or more for a vintage World Series championship ring engraved with the name of a major superstar. While few can afford to amass a collection of rare sports rings, collectors often want to share in the success of their favorite teams by owning a ring from their heroes' most recent championship season.

CHAPTER 9

TICKETS, PROGRAMS, AND PUBLICATIONS

Got a ticket stub from an old Super Bowl game? Did you save your game program from the World Series? Have you ever put away an old newspaper with a historic sports headline across the top? Then you have a valuable piece of sports memorabilia in your collection. The demand for original game tickets, programs, sports magazines, media guides, and old newspapers with historic sports pages has been growing steadily over the past decade. Many collectors, no longer challenged by completing card sets, have turned to the more difficult task of finding rare printed material to diversify their collections.

Several factors go into determining the value of these nostalgic souvenirs. The significance of the event and the overall condition of the item are the most critical factors. When collecting newspapers and magazines, the placement of the headline is important. Is it on the front page or inside in the sports section? Is it accompanied by a photograph? Did you save the complete edition or just the sports section? Is the athlete pictured on the cover of the magazine or is he relegated to a few inside pages?

Super Bowl tickets are prized collectibles

All of these criteria affect the value of an item, but in recent years, as the demand grows and the supply diminishes, the value of all limited collectibles continues to appreciate.

Ticket stubs and programs from any of the World Series games, past Super Bowls, All-Star games, baseball and football league championship games, NBA and NHL finals, world championship boxing matches, past Olympic Games, the Masters, U.S. and British Open golf championships, major college football bowl games, and the NCAA basketball finals all command big bucks in the sports memorabilia market. Although there are no official price guides for old tickets and game programs, you can get an idea of their value by reading the advertisements in various hobby publications such as

Ticket from playoff games are rising in value

Sports Collectors Digest, each issue of which usually contains ads for some of these unusual collectibles.

Ticket stubs from past World Series games can cost as much as $400 or more for pre-1930 games to under $10 for more recent games. A ticket stub from the first baseball All-Star game recently sold for $375. Unused game tickets from past Super Bowl games cost from $200 for the most recent game to over $1,000 for an unused ticket to Super Bowl III, the year the underdog AFL champion New York Jets upset the heavily favored NFL champion Baltimore Colts. Unused tickets from Super Bowls played in the 1970s cost from $400 to $700 each; those from the 1980s, $300 to $500. Ticket stubs from these games will range from 30 percent to 40 percent of the value of a complete unused game ticket.

Game programs from these events also have significant value in the secondary market. World Series programs printed before 1920 command the highest prices, between $1,500 and $10,000, depending on the participating teams and the condition of the program. World Series programs from

Green Bay Packers game program, valued at $125

the 1920s and 1930s cost from $375 to $3,000. The 1933 All-Star game program is valued at around $2,500. Since these prices are beyond the range of most collectors, it is nice to know you can start a World Series program collection starting with the 1970 Series for as little as $75. Subsequent World Series programs range in price from $20 to $75.

Super Bowl programs in mint condition are among the hottest collectibles in the hobby right now. Prices range from $125 to $500 for programs from the first ten Super Bowls. Beginning with Super Bowl X, the NFL began printing a "home edition" of the actual game program and sold it to a mass audience via television commercials and print advertisements. These Super Bowl programs differ slightly from the actual game programs sold at the Super Bowl stadium site and are worth just a fraction of what the real game programs are worth. Actual game programs from Super Bowl XI through the most recent Super Bowl range from $100 to $15. Programs from the NBA Finals are also increasing in popularity along with the sport. NBA championship programs from the 1960s and

Vancouver Canucks game program, worth $25

Sports Illustrated *cover, featuring Mohammad Ali, valued at $125*

1970s cost from $250 for the earlier ones to $100 for the 1979–80 championship series.

Media guides or press guides from professional teams are also highly valued collectibles. Each year teams print media guides full of biographical data and statistics that the press refer to when compiling data for their articles and feature stories. The low production run on these media guides makes them highly sought-after collectibles. Media guides for special events like championship games are rapidly appreciating in value. Super Bowl media guides cost from $40 for the most recent ones to $350 for Super Bowls I and II. Regular season team media guides for Major League Baseball teams and NFL teams are priced from $200 or more for those printed in the 1940s to as little as $6 for those printed in the last five years.

These days, many teams in all sports print their own team yearbooks, which they sell to the public. However, many baseball and football clubs have been producing team yearbooks for more than sixty years. These yearbooks cost from $500 or more for vintage publications to under $10 for recent editions. Official team publications increase in value when the cover subject reaches legendary status or

MOST VALUABLE
***SPORTS ILLUSTRATED* MAGAZINES**

May 19, 1949	Joe DiMaggio cover	$500
August 23, 1954	1954 Topps Yankees	400
August 16, 1954	Eddie Mathews cover	350
August 1, 1955	Ted Williams cover	175
June 18, 1956	Mickey Mantle cover	160
April 11, 1955	Willie Mays cover	130
August 15, 1978	25th Anniversary	100
March 4, 1957	Mickey Mantle cover	100
April 18, 1955	Al Rosen cover	90
June 10, 1963	Cassius Clay cover	75
July 2, 1962	Mickey Mantle cover	75
June 21, 1965	Mickey Mantle cover	70
October 2, 1961	Roger Maris cover	65

the team wins a championship at the end of the year in which the yearbook was produced.

Old sports magazines or vintage general interest magazines with a specific sports theme are some of the most wanted collectibles in the hobby. *Sports Illustrated* magazines are among the most popular but by no means the only sports-related publication that collectors seek out. *The Sporting News*, *Sport Magazine*, and annual baseball, football, and basketball yearbooks published by such companies as Street and Smith have been increasing in value over the years. Popular or once-popular magazines, such as *Life*, *Saturday Evening Post*, *Colliers*, and other general interest periodicals, have value if they have a sports-centered cover or a sports-related feature on the inside pages. Some of these magazines, including many editions of older hobby publications, inserted trading cards between their pages. These publications continue to appreciate in value

Sports magazines increase in value depending on cover subject and overall condition

as long as the magazine remains in mint condition and the insert cards are still intact.

Many of the most historic moments in sports have been immortalized in black and white on the front pages of your daily newspaper. The headlines, the stories, the photographs, all capture the most important events in a team's history or a player's career. Like fine art, historic vintage newspapers

Chicago Daily Tribune

2 SOX CONFESS; 8 INDICTED

SECRECY VEILS TERMS OF U.S. SENT TO TOKIO

GRAND AND PETIT MANDATES

BRITAIN DENIES CONNIVANCE AT ERIN REPRISALS

Eight Fired by Comiskey; Wrecks Team

CICOTTE AND JACKSON ADMIT THROWING SERIES

Chicago Tribune *headline chronicles Black Sox scandal*

DAILY NEWS

NEW YORK'S PICTURE NEWSPAPER

10¢

715!

HENRY DOES IT

Breaks Ruth's Home Run Record

New York Daily News *announces Hank Aaron's record-breaking home run*

always seem to appreciate in value because they are extremely difficult to find in good condition. Front page headlines announcing Don Larsen's perfect game in the 1956 World Series (*New York Herald Tribune*, $350) or Shoeless Joe Jackson's confession regarding the 1919 Chicago Black Sox scandal (*Chicago Tribune*, $2,500) are among the rarest collectibles in the hobby. Headlines heralding Babe

RUTH CLOUTS HOMER, BREAKS OLD MARK

Los Angeles Examiner Sports

WHAT NOTS

BABE POUNDS 60TH, PASSES 1921 RECORD

FAVOR TROJANS OVER BRONCOS AT COLISEUM

Tom Hughes Victor Over Goldstein

Babe Ruth makes the front page of L.A. Herald Examiner

Ruth's sixtieth home run in 1927 (*New York World*, $750) or Roger Maris's sixty-first home run in 1961 (*New York Daily News*, $750) are always in demand.

These headlines capture some of the most important dates in sports. But no matter what the sporting event, there is probably a market for the newspaper account. Reports on Super Bowls, college football bowl games, and championship boxing matches are highly collectible. So are articles about major golf tournaments, the Kentucky Derby, the Indianapolis 500, and the Olympic Games. Most newspapers with a banner headline on these events can be bought for $40 to $100. Collectors often frame these headlines and hang them on a wall to relive a special moment in the history of their favorite team or an important milestone in the career of their favorite player. If a photograph is included in the account of the event, many collectors try to get an autograph from the player. If you plan to collect old newspapers with historic themes, never laminate the newspaper. Instead, have it framed in glass or Plexiglas and keep it in an area that gets little, if any, exposure to the sun.

Sports NEW YORK Herald Tribune TV-Radio

Larsen Hurls 1st Perfect Series Game; Yanks Beat Maglie, 2-0, and Lead 3-2

Only Ford, Cerv Miss Final Out

2 Plays Save No-Hitter; No Dodger Gets to First

Mantle Hits Homer, His 3d in Series

Score of 5th Game

Don Larsen's perfect World Series game reported by the New York Herald Tribune

CHAPTER 10

COINS, STAMPS, ENVELOPES, AND CACHETS

The sports memorabilia hobby, which came into its own only in the second half of this century, is a mere infant compared to coin and stamp collecting, which have been around for centuries. But the field of sports collectibles is no longer considered a stepchild by other collectors. In fact, the rising value of sports memorabilia has brought a lot of coin and stamp collectors into the field and a lot of their grading and conditioning guidelines have been adapted by sports collectors.

Manufacturers of sports collectibles have often borrowed freely from coin and stamp producers, creating myriad sports-related coins and collectible stamps. Many of the old baseball coins in the secondary market today were originally produced as food issues, premiums that were given away free with various food products such as hot dogs, soft drinks, potato chips, tea, and ice cream. In the early 1960s,

Salada Tea Company produced two series of baseball coins, a plastic set consisting of 221 coins in 1962, valued at over $600 today, and a metal set in 1960 consisting of sixty-three coins, worth close to $300 today. Between 1955 and 1960, Armour Franks issued a series of sixty-four coins in its hot dog packages. Today, those coins are worth up to $15 each, with coins of Hall of Famers selling in the $50 range.

The Topps Company produced baseball coins in 1964, 1971, 1987, and 1988, which it used as inserts in baseball card packs. The 1964 set includes 120 regular coins and forty-four All-Star coins. Today, the complete set, in near-mint condition, is valued at over $1,000. The 1971 set consists of 153 coins valued at over $500. There has been little demand for the forty-five-coin 1987 set or the sixty-coin 1988 set, which sell for around $10 to $15 per set in mint condition.

Despite the low demand for recent Topps baseball coins, two new companies have found a niche in the hobby, producing metal coins and commemorative medallions and have done quite well in recent years. Chicagoland Processing Environmint has produced over a hundred different limited commemorative silver and gold medallions since

Limited edition Nolan Ryan coins rising in value

Walter Payton was the subject of a popular coin

1985, which range in value from $750 to $35. A silver coin commemorating Tom Seaver's 300th win and limited to 377 coins is the most valuable at $750, and a silver twelve-coin 1992 USA Basketball set limited to 750 sets is valued at $700. Other coins commemorate World Series highlights, All-Star games, Super Bowl champions, MVPs, Hall of Fame inductees, and special occasions such as Nolan Ryan's retirement.

The Highland Mint, which produces limited metal versions of popular baseball cards, has also issued a series of silver coins honoring individual superstars in each sport. These coins are limited to a run of between 5,000 to 7,500 each and are valued between $30 and $75.

Stamps with sports-related themes are another popular sports collectible. Everyone from Topps to the U.S. Postal Service to several Caribbean countries has issued stamps honoring legendary sports figures. Topps issued its first baseball stamp collection in 1961, with 208 stamps depicting some of the top baseball stars of the day. Two stamps were inserted into each Topps baseball pack and the company also offered an album by mail. Today, a complete set of 1961 Topps baseball stamps is valued at $300 in near-mint condition. The 1962 set contains 200 stamps and sells for over $250 in near-mint condition. The 1969 stamps were issued in team sets and came with twenty-four separate albums, one for each major league team. Today,

Highland Mint produces limited edition commemorative coins

the complete 1969 set is valued at over $300. In 1974, Topps printed ten stamps for each team which could be pasted into individual team albums. The complete 1974 set sells for around $125 today.

Over the years, several companies have produced baseball and football stickers. While they are just as collectible as stamps, they fall into a separate category of sports novelty products. Topps has produced baseball stickers on and off since 1967, when it tested the product with two extremely scarce thirty-three-sticker team issues for the Boston Red Sox and the Pittsburgh Pirates. Each of those team sets is valued in the $350 range today. The following year, Topps produced a set of All-Star stickers

Several Caribbean countries issue commemorative postage stamps

which it tested in selected markets. The lack of national distribution has increased the value of the complete set of sixteen strips with three stickers per strip to over $1,500. In recent years, a European company called Panini has produced a series of collectible stickers which come with an album. Those stickers have slowly appreciated in value, but, as with most stamps and stickers, the investment potential in the long run is better if they are not pasted into albums and are stored in small, clear plastic stamp envelopes or plastic baggies.

In 1989, The U.S. Postal Service issued a four-stamp Legends of Baseball series featuring Roberto Clemente, Lou Gehrig, Jackie Robinson, and Babe Ruth. The stamps were sold in post offices around the country and came with commemorative baseball cards and a brochure. The stamps carried a face value of 20 cents postage and were so popular the Postal Service issued a second printing, diminishing the overall value of the set. Today those stamps are worth around $1 each.

In recent years, several Caribbean countries have found a unique way to raise money by issuing actual postage stamps depicting legendary sports stars or commemorating special sporting events. Used as actual postage within their countries, the stamps have become collector's items in the United States. Guyana and St. George are just two of the countries to cash in on this segment of the hobby

Limited edition Michael Jordan cachet

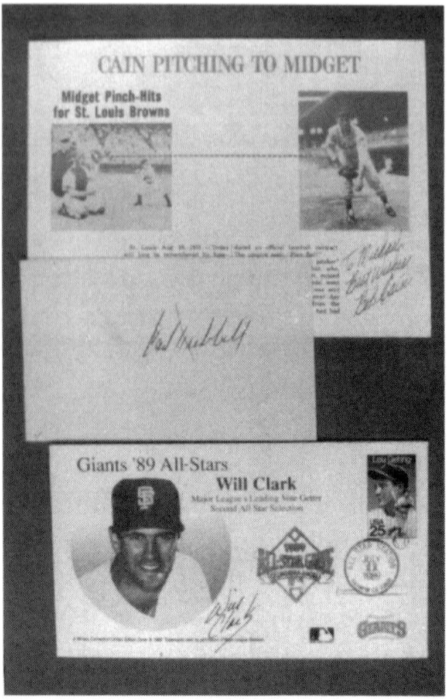

Will Clark is the subject of a limited edition postcard

by producing stamps featuring Roberto Clemente, Jackie Robinson, and Super Bowl commemoratives. These stamps may serve as legal tender in their countries, but they have not appreciated as much as collectors had hoped here in the United States.

One of the more unusual collectibles in the hobby is the first day cachet or collectible envelopes that are used to commemorate a sports milestone or special event. A lot of these envelopes will have original artwork on the front or a unique stamp affixed to them and will carry a postmark with the date of the event and the city in which the event was held. In many cases, dealers of "First Day" issues will have the player sign a limited number of envelopes before the event and then sell autographed versions complete with an authentic postmark with the date and site of the event. Again, there is no price guide available for these original envelopes and prices vary depending on the number of total envelopes in each issue, the status of the player involved, and whether or not the envelope is autographed. However, most of the cachets and commemorative envelopes are limited to between a

Envelope honors Joe Montana

handful and a few thousand, and are usually considered extremely rare. Hall of Fame inductions with Cooperstown, New York, or Canton, Ohio, postmarks are extremely popular collectibles. Retirements, Super Bowls, and All-Star games are other events for which commemorative envelopes are produced. Though the demand for such items is very low, they usually maintain their value and often appreciate in value, duc to their scarcity relative to more popular collectibles.

CHAPTER 11

SPORTS FIGURINES AND STATUES

Some people call them toys, others refer to them as dolls. Many collectors consider them rare and limited works of art. Collectors who are passionate about sports figurines call them gold. That is because no other segment of the hobby has grown as fast as the sports figurine market. The figurines can be found in plastic, papier mâché, ceramics, and even bronze.

From novelty products like Bobbin' Heads and toys like Kenner's Starting Lineup statues to the more artistic sculptures by Gartlan USA, Sports Impressions, Salvino Sports Legends, Hartland, and Sports Accessories and Memorabilia (SAM), sports-themed figurines and statues are appreciating faster than most sports collectibles.

Bobbin' Heads

Except for some rare, one-of-a-kind bronze sculptures of legendary players that have made their way into the secondary market, the first mass-market sports figurines were produced in Japan and imported to the United States in the early 1960s. Made of papier mâché, these

Bronze statue of Babe Ruth with Lou Gehrig

Original Pittsburgh Pirates Bobbin' Head doll from 1961, valued at $1,200 to $1,500

funny-looking toys were called Bobbin' Heads. When they were first issued, they sold for a couple of bucks each and were considered nothing more than novelty products, often given as gag gifts and relegated to a sports fan's bookshelf or desk. Occasionally you might see a Bobbin' Head staring out at you from the rear window of an automobile, neck bouncing over every pothole and head twisting with every turn in the road. Today, because of their relative scarcity and a growing demand for the odd little dolls, some Bobbin' Heads are worth hundreds of dollars, with a few topping the $1,000 mark.

Between 1960 and 1972, a total of 175 different Bobbin' Head dolls were produced, seventy-eight baseball, eighty football, ten hockey, and seven basketball. A number of rare and extremely scarce mini-versions were also created and distributed over this same twelve-year period. In many cases, mini-versions are valued at two to three times the price of the regular issues. There were also many variations of the original dolls, with some players appearing on both round and square bases. Long-time collectors have been able to determine the age and scarcity of many of the original Bobbin' Heads by researching the shape, size, and color of the base. Some of the early Bobbin' Heads are generic team dolls with heads that do not resemble any particular player. Other variations consist of team dolls with both white-skinned and dark-skinned faces, the dark-skinned ones being scarcer and thus more valuable.

Because Bobbin' Heads are lightweight papier mâché products, they are easily damaged; as with most sports memorabilia, the condition of each doll plays a major role in determining its value. Collectors should check for cracks and chips, especially along the base of the doll. Slight damage can decrease the value of a Bobbin' Head doll by 40 percent to 50 percent. Occasionally a collector may come upon a Bobbin' Head doll that has been repaired. A few unscrupulous dealers have become

Bobbin' Head figurines, first produced in the 1960s, are among the most valuable collectibles in the hobby today

adept at patching up the cracks, repainting the dolls, and passing them off as mint. In many cases, the color of the doll's base determines its scarcity and, in a few instances, dealers have repainted the base, changing its more common color to a rarer, more valuable one. If you are determined to buy one of the more expensive dolls, you may want to get a second opinion or ask for a money-back guarantee. Most dealers will gladly refund your money if you can prove the doll has been doctored in any way.

The recent resurgence in interest in the older Bobbin' Head dolls has created a market for a new, taller, modern version. Since 1991, a company called Sports Accessories and Memorabilia (SAM) has manufactured limited-edition, nine-inch versions of Bobbin' Heads, featuring such current superstars as Michael Jordan, Ken Griffey Jr., and Jerry Ric, legends like Joe Montana, Larry Bird, and Nolan Ryan, and Hall of Famers like Mickey Mantle, Babe Ruth, Willie Mays, and Roger Staubach. Production of each new Bobbin' Head is limited to 3,000 per player and the market values for the newer models range from $40 to $175.

One of the first American producers of sports

MOST VALUABLE BOBBIN' HEAD FIGURINES*

1963 Roberto Clemente (caricature)	$1,500
1962 Pittsburgh Pirates (white base)	1,200
1963 Mickey Mantle (caricature)	650
1963 Willie Mays (gold base)	550
1962 Dallas Texans (AFL)	550
1962 New York Titans (AFL)	550
1968 Houston Astros (gold base)	500
1962 Houston Oilers (AFL)	500
1963 Roger Maris (caricature)	475
1962 Boston Bruins	450
1960 Washington Senators (blue base)	400
1968 Washington Redskins	400

* Mini-versions valued at approximately twice the price of the regular issues

figurines was the Hartland Company. From 1960 through 1963 the company produced an extremely limited number of handsculpted statues of some of the era's top baseball stars. These realistic figurines were often limited to between fifteen and 150 per player and are very difficult to find in today's secondary market. The most valuable is a 1961 statue of former National League MVP Dick Groat of the Pittsburgh Pirates. Only thirty-five statues of Groat are known to exist today and sell for around $2,200 each. Hartland turned out fifty Rocky Colavito statues in the early 1960s that are worth around $1,200 each today. Hartland statues of Hank Aaron, Ernie Banks, Yogi Berra, Mickey Mantle, Roger Maris, Eddie Mathews, Willie Mays, Stan Musial, and Ted Williams are valued in the $300 to $650 range and continue to appreciate annually.

Starting Lineup Figurines

Some of the most successful sports collectibles issued in recent years are the Kenner Starting Lineup figurines, which have become the most popular sports statues in America. Former Cincinnati Bengals punter Pat McInally saw the popularity of such mythical action figures as GI Joe and figured kids would like to play with real-life action figures of the sports stars of the day. In 1988, Kenner, an Ohio-based toy company, embraced the idea and issued a 124-piece baseball set with indi-

Starting Lineup figurines continue to appreciate in value

vidual baseball figurines selling for under $5 each. Today, the five-inch plastic figurines have gone from popular toys to valuable collectibles, having caught on with collectors of all ages.

The phenomenal growth of Starting Lineup can be attributed to several factors. The figurines were packaged with a collectible sports card or a coin, which added value to the product. Individual statues were produced in limited quantities and production numbers often varied from player to player. Starting Lineup figurines were at first distributed regionally, with certain players available only in the markets surrounding their home teams. This distribution method made it easy for collectors in New England to buy Red Sox statues, but it was nearly impossible for them to find statues of Dodgers or Giants players. Basketball figurines of Utah Jazz players are the scarcest and the most valuable.

Soon dealers began to set up networks where collectors could trade extra statues from their regions for statues that were not available in their areas. A small subculture of Starting Lineup fanatics grew and the values for the figurines began to

Carl Yastzremski Starting Lineup figurine, originally sold for under $4 and is now worth over $65

soar. Today, the complete 124-piece 1988 Starting Lineup baseball set is valued at around $3,000, with some individual statues selling for over $400 each.

Since introducing the line in 1988, Kenner has produced more than 1,500 different Starting Lineup figurines covering all four major sports. To keep the concept fresh, the company produced several specially themed editions such as Headliners (1991), which featured only superstars and came with a walnut-like base and included a newspaper clipping of the player's major accomplishments. The company has also produced such special editions as Baseball Greats; Baseball, Football and Basketball Legends; One-On-Ones, which featured two players per base; and Stadium Stars, which

MOST VALUABLE STARTING LINEUP FIGURINES

1988	Karl Malone	$450
1988	Nolan Ryan	325
1988	John Stockton	275
1988	Cal Ripken Jr.	250
1988	Joe Montana	225
1989	Michael Jordan w/Larry Bird	200
1989	Michael Jordan w/Isaiah Thomas	200
1992	Magic Johnson	200
1988	Dan Marino	180
1988	Jerry Rice	175
1988	Tony Dorsett	150
1989	Steve Young	150
1991	Emmitt Smith	150
1988	Art Monk	140
1988	Jim Kelly	140

consisted of large figurines standing on models of their home stadiums.

Starting Lineup figurines have become so popular with collectors that memorabilia conventions devoted exclusively to plastic statues have sprouted up around the country. These regional events can attract several thousand Starting Lineup collectors who are devoted to completing entire sets. Kenner recently started a newsletter to keep Starting Lineup collectors informed of new releases and convention news, and several hobby price guides now include current values for Starting Lineup figurines.

OTHER FIGURINES AND STATUES

The growing popularity of sports figurines has prompted several new companies to jump on the bandwagon. Since the mid-1980s, three companies have introduced limited edition sports figurines, most of which measure between seven and ten inches high, with each company adding its own special features. Many of the newer editions are autographed by the player depicted on the statue.

Gartland USA has been producing figurines since 1985. Most its figurines are limited to quantities that range between 1,089 and 2,650, and most have been autographed by the player. A limited figurine of Magic Johnson, signed by Johnson, is considered the most valuable Gartland statue, worth over $2,500. Only 250 of them are known to be in circulation. Wayne Gretzky's autographed Gartland figurine (limited to 1,851 statues) is valued at over $1,000. Ted Williams' is valued at $750, Kareem Abdul Jabbar's goes for around $600, and Carl Yastzremski's fetches $500. Gartland also produced mini-versions of its figurines in quantities of around 10,000 per player. Those figurines cost between $40 and $50 today.

A company called Sports Impressions has produced sports figurines in various sizes and quantities since 1987. Quantities range from around 950 per player to as many as 5,750 per player. Today those statues command from $100 to $300 in the secondary market.

In 1988, Salvino Sports Legends became a major manufacturer of popular sports figurines, most limited to between 500 and 2,000 per player and most autographed by the player. Salvino figurines are valued at between $150 and $700, depending on the player and the total production; Mario Lemieux's figurine is the most valuable, at around $700.

Collectors interested in exploring the sports figurine market can find dealers who specialize in figurines at most large baseball card shows and memorabilia conventions. Statues like Starting Lineups and Bobbin' Heads are sold in toy departments at most major department and discount stores. Smaller companies use an exclusive network of hobby dealers or sell their original figurines by mail order. Check the pages of some of the major hobby publications for advertisements that coincide with the release of each new figurine.

Bobbin' Head dolls are making a comeback in the 1990s

CHAPTER 12

MISCELLANEOUS ITEMS

Whoever coined the phrase, "One man's trash is another man's treasure" could have easily been a sports collector. Sports memorabilia encompasses myriad unusual items, from commemorative bottles and cans to plastic cups and glasses, from cereal boxes and advertising signs to old baseball board games and original limited edition works of art. If the item has a sports-related theme, chances are there is a market for it.

For decades, soft drink companies and regional breweries have honored championship teams or individual sports achievements by producing commemorative packaging. These limited edition bottles or cans may include a picture of a team or a player on the front along with a banner proclaiming the achievement or milestone. Most of these items are distributed regionally, usually in the market where the team or player is based. The value for such items is usually determined by the event or milestone, the player, and the age and condition of the collectible. The scarcity of such items does not affect their value as much as demand does, and the demand for old bottles and cans is low, relative to the more popular autographed items profiled in this book. Although the segment of the hobby that collects such items is small, old bottles and cans have sold for more than $100. Unopened bottles or cans are worth

Commemorative beer cans are popular collectibles

Wine label marking Babe Ruth's 100th birthday makes a nice souvenir but has no value in secondary market

Wheaties honors NFL's 75th Anniversary with commemorative package

more than opened containers. However, old aluminum or metal cans that contain a carbonated beverage may deteriorate over time. The best way to preserve them is to open the cans from the bottom, drain and rinse them, and store them in a cool, dry place.

Convenience stores and gasoline stations often give away collectible plastic cups or glasses with the purchase of soft drinks or gasoline. These promotional items make nice collectibles, but are rarely worth big bucks. Plastic baseball and football cups issued by 7-Eleven back in the early 1970s are worth from 25 cents to $10 each, depending on the player who is pictured on the cup. Although many of these older souvenirs are extremely difficult to find, the demand for them is low, which keeps the value down.

Over the years, Wheaties has honored championship teams and a few select superstars by printing their pictures on cereal boxes. Many of the commemorative Wheaties boxes were issued regionally around the city where the championship team is based. Since these boxes are considered rather limited, there is a growing market for old Wheaties boxes. Wheaties boxes with commemo-

Commemorative Wheaties boxes range in value from $25 to $75

Original lithographs are more valuable when signed and numbered by the artist

Limited edition art honors Los Angeles Lakers championship season

rative sports themes, in mint condition, have sold in the $25 to $50 range. Again, unopened boxes are worth more than opened boxes.

Over the past few years there has also been renewed collector interest in old baseball board games. Toy makers and game manufacturers have been producing various baseball games since the 1920s. Some of these games came with playing cards, dice or a spinner, and a playing board. If the game is intact and the outer box is in excellent to near-mint condition, it probably has some value. Ads for old baseball games have asked prices in the $50 to $100 range. Like many rare items, this col-

Baseball art cards and limited edition postcards are rising in value

lectible is worth only what someone is willing to pay for it.

One of the fastest growing segments of the hobby is limited edition sports art. The popularity of the art is usually based on the subject or celebrity pictured, the skill and reputation of the artist, and the scarcity of the artwork. Original lithographs or limited edition prints will also be more valuable if the artwork is signed by the celebrity and then signed and numbered by the artist. Because lithographs and original prints come in all sizes and are reproduced in various quantities, it is nearly impossible to zero in on a range of values. Each piece of art should be appraised individually and, like most original art, is worth only what someone else is willing to pay. Since most of these original prints are produced in limited quantities, it is safe to assume that they should appreciate over time.

CHAPTER 13

CARE AND PRESERVATION

Collectors of sports cards have always known that a tiny scratch, a little crease, or a bent corner can decrease the value of a card. A drop of one grade, say from mint condition to near-mint condition, can reduce the value of a collectible by as much as 50 percent. So they take great care to preserve those valuable cardboard commodities.

Unlike cards, which are usually stored in plastic sheets, binders, or boxes, sports memorabilia is often proudly showcased on bookshelves or framed and displayed on walls. Preserving sports collectibles in the proper holders will go a long way toward maintaining their peak value.

No matter what type of memorabilia you have, there is a holder or display case for it. Enterprising companies have developed products designed to showcase and protect everything from signed baseballs and footballs, to baseball bats, football helmets, basketballs, hockey pucks, game-worn jerseys, and old newspapers and magazines. The best of those products not only offer a convenient way to display memorabilia but also afford maximum visibility and protection.

Ball holders and display cases come in all shapes and sizes. They can be round, square, or dome-shaped. They can be made of plastic,

Individual holders are the best way to display and preserve autographed baseballs

acrylic, or glass. Some have wooden or ceramic bases, others are perfectly clear on all sides, including the bottom. Some glass and Plexiglas holders are slightly tinted to offer protection from harmful ultraviolet rays from the sun. Some holders are stackable, some are wall-mountable, others are both. There are single-size ball holders and wall racks that can hold up to thirty-six baseballs or hockey pucks. Prices for ball holders and display cases range from less than 60 cents for a small, clear plastic golf ball holder to $1,000 or more for a multiple bat display cabinet made of solid wood with a glass front and security lock.

One of the largest suppliers of ball holders is a Nacodoches, Texas, company called Ball Qube, Inc. The company makes plastic containers that are clear on all sides. Although not air-tight or UV-protected, they are easy to open and close, stackable, and affordable. Single baseball holders sell for under $1.50, football and basketball holders range from $25 to $30, and helmet holders for under $50. The company recently introduced a clear plastic bat holder, an adjustable, wall-mountable tube, several of which can be stacked in various configurations. The new bat holders sell for under $30.

Some collectors prefer the globe-shaped ball holders because they offer a little more style. Show-

The best holders offer a 360-degree contact-free view of the baseball

case U.S.A. is a leading distributor of the globe containers, which feature clear plastic tops mounted on a wooden base. They are available in various team colors and make for an attractive display; they cost a little more than the simpler holders.

Mounted Memories, Inc., of Ft. Lauderdale, Florida, bills itself as the largest manufacturer and distributor of acrylic holders and displays in the country, supplying more than 6,000 retail card shops. The company's baseball holders range from $2.50 for a single globe-shaped acrylic top mounted on a wooden base to more elaborate $35 holders. It also offers standard-size holders for footballs, basketballs, hockey pucks, baseball bats, boxing gloves, football helmets, and golf balls. At the top of the line is a wall-mounted jersey display case for around $250, designed to showcase and preserve game-worn uniforms in the same way a museum would display a valuable work of art.

For your most expensive collectibles, you might want to consider the protective products from Premier-Glaser-Bailey, an Escondido, California, company that has earned a reputation for stylish custom-made trophy cases. All of its upscale products are designed to preserve, protect, and showcase valuable sports memorabilia, and from single baseball holders to multiple bat cabinets, the com-

Some collectors mount their memorabilia on wall plaques

pany has managed to integrate design and style into its products. The company's dome-shaped baseball holders are made of glass on either a wood or marble base; wooden ones are made of solid hard woods, no laminates, and marble ones can be custom engraved. Three different tints are available to protect the collectible from ultraviolet exposure. Of course, as a top-of-the-line supplier, Premier-Glaser-Bailey's products aren't cheap: a single baseball holder on a wooden base sells for around $40, engraved; the same holder on a marble base with a bronze engraved plate costs around $70.

The amount you decide to spend on preservation supplies should depend on the value of the collectible—you would not want to preserve a Babe Ruth autographed baseball in a $1.50 plastic holder. There are several other rules to follow for displaying valuable sports memorabilia. The most obvious is to keep the item out of direct sunlight. Never display the item where it is easily accessible to small children. And try to find a balance between what the displayed item is worth and what you want to spend on the holder or display case. If you are constantly adding to your collection, buy stackable

Myriad products are available to protect and display sports memorabilia

holders. And buy holders and display cases that offer maximum protection from humidity, dust, and dirt, as well as full visibility. A rare autographed collectible can bring you a lifetime of enjoyment. The right display holder will not only highlight its contents, it will also protect your investment for future generations to enjoy.

INSTANT EXPERT RESOURCES

CHAPTER 14

Auction Houses

Broadway Rick's Strike Zone
1840 N. Federal Highway
Boynton Beach, FL 33435
800-334-9103

Christie's East,
219 E. 67th Street
New York, NY 10021
212-606-0543

Robert Edward Auctions
P.O. Box 1923
Hoboken, NJ 07030
201-792-9324

Executive Investments Co.
9301 Wilshire Blvd., Ste. 500
Beverly Hills, CA 90210
310-278-1580

Guernsey's,
108 E. 73rd Street
New York, NY 10021
212-794-2280

Hall's Nostalgia
9 Mystic Street, Box 408
Arlington, MA 02174
617-646-7757

Howard's Sports Collectibles
128 E. Main Street
Leipsic, OH 45856
800-457-9974

Leland's
245 Fifth Avenue, Ste. 902
New York, NY 10016
212-545-0800

Greg Manning Auctions Inc.
115 Main Road
Montville, NJ 07045
800-221-0243

Ron Oser Enterprises
P.O. Box 101
Huntington Valley, PA 19006
215-947-6575

Alan Rosen
70 #1 Chesnut Ridge Road
Montvale, NJ 07645
201-307-0700

Kevin Savage Cards
3509 Briarfield Blvd.
Maumee, OH 43537
419-861-2330

Sotheby's
1334 York Avenue
New York, NY 10021
212-606-7000

Spivack & Kraut Inc.
1210 Northbrook Drive, Ste. 405
Trevose, PA 19053
215-953-9960

Sports Collectors Store
1040 S. LaGrange Road
LaGrange, IL 60525
708-354-7970

TeleTrade, P.O. Box 660
Hurley, NY, 12443
800-232-1132

Kit Young
11535 Sorrento Valley Road, Ste. 403
San Diego, CA 92121
619-259-1300

Wolffers
133 Kearny Street, Ste. 400
San Francisco, CA 94108
415-781-5127

MAJOR LEAGUE BASEBALL

Major League Baseball
350 Park Avenue
New York, NY 10022

American League
350 Park Avenue
New York, NY 10022

Baltimore Orioles
333 West Camden Street
Baltimore, MD 21201

Boston Red Sox
4 Yawkey Way
Boston, MA 02215

California Angels
2000 Gene Autry Way
Anaheim, CA 92806

Chicago White Sox
333 W. 35th Street
Chicago, IL 60616

Cleveland Indians
2401 Ontario Street
Cleveland, OH 44115

Detroit Tigers
Tiger Stadium
2121 Trunbull Avenue
Detroit, MI 48216

Kansas City Royals
P.O. Box 419969
Kansas City, MO 64141

Milwaukee Brewers
County Stadium, P.O. Box 3099
Milwaukee, WI 53201

Minnesota Twins
501 Chicago Ave. S.
Minneapolis, MN 55415

New York Yankees
Yankee Stadium
E. 161 St. and River Ave.
Bronx, NY 10451

Oakland Athletics
Oakland Coliseum
7000 Coliseum Way
Oakland, CA 94621

Seattle Mariners
P.O. Box 4100
411 First Ave. S.
Seattle, WA 98104

Texas Rangers
1000 Ballpark Way
Arlington, TX 76011

Toronto Blue Jays
One Blue Jay Way, Ste. 3200
Toronto, Ontario, Canada M5V 1J1

National League
350 Park Ave.
New York, NY 10022

Atlanta Braves
P.O. Box 4064
Atlanta, GA 30302

Chicago Cubs
1060 West Addison Street
Chicago, IL 60613

Cincinnati Reds
100 Riverfront Stadium
Cincinnati, OH 45202

Colorado Rockies
2850 West 20th Ave.
Denver, CO 80211

Florida Marlins
2269 N.W. 199th Street
Miami, FL 33056

Houston Astros
P.O. Box 288
Houston, TX 77001

Los Angeles Dodgers
1000 Elysian Park Ave.
Los Angeles, CA 90012

Montreal Expos
4549 Pierre-de-Coubertin Ave.
Montreal, PQ Canada HI5 3N7

New York Mets
Shea Stadium
Roosevelt Ave. and 126th Street
Flushing, NY 11368

Philadelphia Phillies
P.O. Box 7575
Philadelphia, PA 19101

Pittsburgh Pirates
Three Rivers Stadium
300 Stadium Circle
Pittsburgh, PA 15212

St. Louis Cardinals
250 Stadium Plaza
St. Louis, MO 63102

San Diego Padres
P.O. Box 2000
San Diego, CA 92112

San Francisco Giants
Candlestick Park
San Francisco, CA 94124

NATIONAL BASKETBALL ASSOCIATION

National Basketball Assoc.
Olympic Tower
645 Fifth Ave
New York, NY 10022

Atlanta Hawks
One CNN Center, Ste. 405
Atlanta, GA 30303

Boston Celtics
151 Merrimac Street
Boston, MA 02114

Charlotte Hornets
One Hive Drive
Charlotte, NC 28217

Chicago Bulls
One Magnificent Mile
980 N. Michigan Ave., Ste. 1600
Chicago, IL 60611

Cleveland Cavaliers
The Coliseum
2923 Streetsboro Road
Richfield, OH 44286

Dallas Mavericks
Reunion Arena
777 Sports Street
Dallas, TX 75207

Denver Nuggets
McNichols Sports Arena
1635 Clay Street
Denver, CO 80204

Detroit Pistons
Palace of Auburn Hills
Two Championship Drive
Auburn Hills, MI 48057

Golden State Warriors
Oakland Coliseum
7000 Coliseum Way
Oakland, CA 94621

Houston Rockets
The Summit
Ten Greenway Plaza
Houston, TX 77046

Indiana Pacers
300 E. Market St.
Indianapolis, IN 46204

Los Angeles Clippers
Sports Arena
3939 S. Figueroa Street
Los Angeles, CA 90037

Los Angeles Lakers
Great Western Forum
3900 W. Manchester
Inglewood, CA 90306

Miami Heat
Miami Arena
Miami, FL 33136

Milwaukee Bucks
Bradley Center
1001 N. Fourth Street
Milwaukee, WI 53203

Minnesota Timberwolves
Target Center
600 First Ave. N.
Minneapolis, MN 55403

New Jersey Nets
Brendan Byrne Arena
East Rutherford, NY 07073

New York Knicks
Two Pennsylvania Plaza
New York, NY 10121

Orlando Magic
Orlando Arena
One Magic Place
Orlando, FL 32801

Philadelphia 76ers
Veterans Stadium
P.O. Box 25040
Philadelphia, PA 19147

Phoenix Suns
201 E. Jefferson Street
Phoenix, AZ 85004

Portland Trailblazers
700 N.E. Multnomah Street, Ste. 600
Portland, OR 97232

Sacramento Kings
One Sports Parkway
Sacramento, CA 95834

San Antonio Spurs
600 E. Market Street, Ste. 102
San Antonio, TX 78205

Seattle Supersonics
190 Queen Anne Ave. N., Ste. 200
Seattle, WA 98109

Toronto Raptors
150 York Street, Ste.1100
Toronto, Ontario M5H 355

Utah Jazz
Delta Center
301 West South Temple
Salt Lake City, UT 84101

Vancouver Grizzlies
788 Beatty Street
Vancouver, BC V68 2MI

Washington Bullets
Capital Center
One Harry S. Truman Drive
Landover, MD 20785

National Football League

National Football League
410 Park Ave.
New York, NY 10022

Arizona Cardinals
8701 South Hardy
Tempe, AZ 85284

Atlanta Falcons
Suwanee Rd. at I-85
Suwanee, GA 30175

Buffalo Bills
One Bills Drive
Orchard Park, NY 14127

Carolina Panthers
227 West Trade Street
Charlotte, NC 28202

Chicago Bears
Halas Hall
250 N. Washington Road
Lake Forest, IL 60045

Cincinnati Bengals
200 Riverfront Stadium
Cincinnati, OH 45202

Cleveland Browns
Cleveland Stadium
Cleveland, OH 44114

Dallas Cowboys
Cowboys Center
1 Cowboys Parkway,
Irving, TX 75063

Denver Broncos
13655 East Dove Valley Parkway
Englewood, CO 80112

Detroit Lions
1200 Featherstone Road
Pontiac, MI 48057

Green Bay Packers
1265 Lombardi Ave.
Green Bay, WI 54304

Houston Oilers
6910 Fannin Street
Houston, TX 77030

Indianapolis Colts
7001 W. 56th Street
Indianapolis, IN 46224

Jacksonville Jaguars
One Stadium Place
Jacksonville, FL 32202

Kansas City Chiefs
1 Arrowhead Drive
Kansas City, MO 64129

Miami Dolphins
Joe Robbie Stadium
2269 N.W. 199th Street
Miami, Fl 33056

Minnesota Vikings
9520 Vikings Drive
Eden Prairie, MN 55344

New England Patriots
Foxboro Stadium, Route 1
Foxboro, MA 02035

New Orleans Saints
1500 Poydras Street
New Orleans, LA 70003

New York Giants
Giants Stadium
East Rutherford, NJ 07073

New York Jets
1000 Fulton Ave.
Hempstead, NY 11550

Oakland Raiders
Oakland Coliseum
7000 Coliseum Way
Oakland, CA 94621

Philadelphia Eagles
Broad Street & Pattison Ave.
Philadelphia, PA 19148

Pittsburgh Steelers
Three Rivers Stadium
300 Stadium Circle
Pittsburgh, PA 15212

San Diego Chargers
Jack Murphy Stadium
9449 Friars Road
San Diego, CA 92108

San Francisco 49ers
4949 Centennial Blvd.
Santa Clara, CA 95054

Seattle Seahawks
11220 N.E. 53rd Street
Kirkland, WA 98033

St. Louis Rams
100 N. Broadway, Ste. 2100
St. Louis, MO 63102

Tampa Bay Buccaneers
One Buccaneer Plaza
Tampa, FL 33607

Washington Redskins
P.O. Box 17247
Dulles International Airport
Washington, DC 20041

National Hockey League

National Hockey League
75 International Blvd., Ste. 300
Rexdale, Ontario
Canada M9W 6L9

Anaheim Mighty Ducks
Disney Sports Enterprises, Inc.
P.O. Box 61007, 2695 E. Katella Ave.
Anaheim, CA 92803

Boston Bruins
One Fleet Center, Ste. 250
Boston, MA 02114-1303

Buffalo Sabres
Memorial Auditorium
140 Main Street
Buffalo, NY 14202

Calgary Flames
The SaddleDome
P.O. Box 1540, Station M
Calgary, AB
Canada T2P 3B9

Chicago Blackhawks
1901 W. Madison Street
Chicago, IL 60612

Colorado Avalanche
1635 Clay Street
Denver, CO 80204

Dallas Stars
NationsBank Plaza
901 Main Street, Ste. 2301
Dallas, TX 75202

Detroit Red Wings
Joe Louis Arena
600 Civic Center Drive
Detroit, MI 48226

Edmonton Oilers
Northlands Coliseum
Edmonton, AB
Canada, T5B 4M9

Florida Panthers
110 N.E. 3rd Ave., 10th Floor
Ft. Lauderdale, FL 33301

Hartford Whalers
242 Trumbull Dr., 8th Floor
Hartford, CT 06013

Los Angeles Kings
3900 W. Manchester Blvd.
P.O. Box 10
Inglewood, CA 90308

Montreal Canadians
Montreal Forum
2313 St. Catherine Street W.
Montreal, PQ
Canada H3H 1N2

New Jersey Devils
Byrne Meadowlands Arena
P.O. Box 504
East Rutherford, NJ 07073

New York Islanders
Nassau Coliseum
Uniondale, NY 11553

New York Rangers
Madison Square Garden
4 Pennsylvania Plaza
New York, NY 10001

Ottawa Senators
301 Moodie Drive, Ste. 200
Nepean, Ontario
Canada K2H 9C4

Philadelphia Flyers
The Spectrum
Pattison Place
Philadelphia, PA 19148

Pittsburgh Penguins
Civic Arena
Pittsburgh, PA 15219

San Jose Sharks
525 W. Santa Clara Street
San Jose, CA 95113

St. Louis Blues
St. Louis Arena
5700 Oakland Ave.
St. Louis, MO 63110

Tampa Bay Lightning
1 Mack Center
501 E. Kennedy Blvd., Ste. 175
Tampa, FL 33602

Toronto Maple Leafs
Maple Leaf Gardens
60 Carlton Street
Toronto, Ontario
Canada M5B 1L1

Vancouver Canucks
Pacific Coliseum
100 N. Renfrew Street
Vancouver, BC
Canada V5K 3N7

Winnipeg Jets
Winnipeg Arena
15-1430 Maroons Road
Winnipeg, Manitoba
Canada R3G 0L5

HALLS OF FAME

Hockey Hall of Fame
BCE Place
30 Yonge Street
Toronto, Ontario
Canada M5E 1X8

International Boxing Hall of Fame
1 Hall of Fame Drive
P.O. Box 425
Canastota, NY 13032

International Hockey Hall of Fame and Museum
P.O. Box 82, York & Alfred Streets
Kingston, Ontario
Canada K7L 4V6

Naismath Memorial Basketball Hall of Fame
1150 W. Columbus Ave.
Springfield, MA 01101

National Baseball Hall of Fame and Museum
P.O. Box 590
Cooperstown, NY 13326

Pro Football Hall of Fame
2121 George Halas Drive, N.W.
Canton, OH 44708

United States Hockey Hall of Fame
P.O. Box 657, Hat Trick Ave.
Eveleth, MN 55734

HOBBY PUBLICATIONS

Beckett Baseball Card Monthly
P.O. Box 2048
Marion, OH 43305

Encyclopedia of Sports Memorabilia
9171 Wilshire Blvd, Ste. 300
Beverly Hills, CA 90210

Sports Card Trader
P.O. Box 433
Mt. Morris, IL 61054

Sports Collectors Digest
700 East State St.
Iola, WI 54990

Trading Cards
P.O. Box 16928
N. Hollywood, CA 91615

Tuff Stuff
P.O. Box 1637
Glen Allen, VA 23060

CHAPTER 15

TALK LIKE AN EXPERT

GLOSSARY OF TERMS

Ask Price—The selling price asked by a dealer, investor, or collector.

Autographed Item—Any sports collectible signed by a player, such as a ball, bat, glove, photograph, program, scorecard, artwork, uniform.

Bid Price—The buy price offered by a dealer, investor, or collector.

Book Price—A price guide listing of the current retail value of a sports card or autographed sports collectible.

Buy Price—The price a dealer is willing to pay for a sports collectible. It is usually substantially lower than the listed price guide value in order for the dealer to make a profit when the item is resold.

Card Lot—A group of identical single cards packaged in "lots" of 10, 25, 50, 100 or more and sold for less than the total values of the individual cards.

Case—A container of wax or foil boxes of sports cards usually sold at wholesale prices to dealers, retailers, or discount warehouses.

Chipping—A defect found on a card or collectible that can affect the grade of the item. Chipping refers to a scratch on an item in which the color or paint is worn away.

Condition—The amount of wear and tear of a collectible, a major factor in determining its value.

Convention—A event that brings together collectors, memorabilia dealers, and, on occasion, memorabilia manufacturers to buy, sell, trade, and promote sports cards and sports memorabilia. Usually held in convention centers, hotel meeting rooms, community centers, or gymnasiums, an admission fee is often charged.

Counterfeits—A phony item reproduced to look like an original collectible or a fake signature made to look like a player's autograph. Counterfeit sports collectibles have no value and in many states it is a felony to produce, distribute, or sell them.

Dealer—A person who buys, sells, and trades sports cards and sports memorabilia, either full-time or part-time, for profit.

Error Cards (ER)—Sports cards with such mistakes as misspellings, erroneous statistics or biographical data, or a wrong photograph or other graphics. Most error cards have no significant value unless a corrected card is issued creating a variation. (See Variations.)

Exhibit Postcards—Picture postcards, usually black and white or sepia, featuring sports celebrities and entertainers produced by the Exhibit Supply Company, Chicago, Illinois, and sold in penny arcade machines from the 1920s to the 1960s.

Facsimile Autograph—A signature on a card or sports collectible that has been reproduced during the manufacturing process and is incorporated into its overall design.

Food Issues—Sports cards and collectibles given away as premiums in food products such as candy, cereal, cookies, hot dogs, ice cream, meat products, or potato chips. Food products that offer sports collectibles as part of a mail-in promotion would also qualify as food issues.

Game-Worn—Describes a uniform or part of a uniform such as a jersey that was worn by a player during a regular season, post-season, or all-star game.

Goudey—A Boston-based gum company that produced sports cards from 1933 to 1939.

Grade—A subjective analysis of the physical condition of a sports collectible used to arrive at the value of an item.

Grading Service—A company that specializes in the analysis of the condition and authenticity of a particular sports card or collectible. For a fee, the company will assign a grade and assign a letter of authenticity.

Letter of Authenticity—A certificate guaranteeing that the sports collectible being sold is genuine.

Limited Edition—A sports collectible produced in small quantities and often numbered, such as 1 of 2,000 or 1 of 700.

Mail Bids—An advertised auction of sports cards or memorabilia in which bids are mailed to the advertiser. The product is then sold to the highest bidder.

Mint—The highest grade on the condition scale; a sports card or sports collectible in perfect condition without a single flaw.

Old Judge—A set of baseball cards, classified as a tobacco issue, produced between 1887 and 1890 and deriving its name from Old Judge Cigarettes, which issued the cards as a premium.

Panel—An uncut sheet containing two or more sports cards.

Plastic Sheet—A product made of clear plastic or polyvinyl used to store and preserve cards. The most popular ones contain nine pockets.

Press Run—The total amount of card sets produced for any particular edition of sports cards.

Price Guide—A magazine or book that contains a checklist of cards or a listing of autographed sports memorabilia, along with their current values.

Replica Jersey—A brand new team jersey produced by a licensed manufacturer, designed to look like an original team jersey and sold in department, discount, and sporting goods stores.

Reprints—Reproductions of original cards or collectibles that are usually scarce or limited. Most are labeled as reprints and have very little value.

Scarce—Denotes a card or collectible that is extremely difficult to find in the secondary market.

Secondary Market—The market for non-current and older sports memorabilia that has changed hands since its initial release and is bought and sold by collectors and dealers at card shops or at card shows and conventions.

Sell Price—The price for which a dealer is willing to sell a sports card or collectible. In most cases, sell prices are much higher than buy prices.

Series—A group of cards or collectibles that are part of a set but issued in smaller groups until the entire set has been distributed.

Set—The complete production run of a particular edition of cards or sports collectibles.

Test Issue—A limited set of cards or collectibles produced to test-market a new concept or design. Usually distributed in limited geographical areas.

Tobacco Issues—Cards and collectibles such as pins, used as premiums in cigarette packages starting in the late 1880s. They may contain a picture of a sports figure on one side and an advertising message on the flip side. They carry the "T" designation in price guides and are among the most valuable in the hobby.

Uncut Sheet—A sheet of cards from a press run before the cards have been individually cut into single cards.

Variation—Means that at least two versions of the same card or collectible exist. This usually happens when an error is corrected in future production runs and then put into circulation by the manufacturer. In some cases, both the original error card and the variation will become more valuable because both have been produced in lesser quantities than the other cards in the same set.

Vintage Material—Generally refers to sports memorabilia produced and issued prior to 1970.

Want List—A list of sports cards and memorabilia compiled by a collector or a dealer who is looking to buy the listed items.

CHAPTER 16

INSTANT EXPERT QUIZ

Questions

1 What player's game-worn jersey sold for a record $363,000 at auction?

2 What is the name for an autograph applied to a collectible during the manufacturing process?

3 What former NFL player invented the Starting Lineup figurines?

4 When did numbers first appear on baseball uniforms?

5 Press pins ordered by playoff teams who fail to make it to the World Series are called what?

6 In 1989, the U.S. Postal Service honored four legendary players with commemorative stamps. Name them.

7 Who is pictured on the cover of the most valuable *Sports Illustrated* Magazine?

8 What do you call sports collectibles given away with products such as cereal, cookies, ice cream, hot dogs, and potato chips?

9 The most valuable single-signed basketball contains what player's signature?

10 What major league baseball team commissioned the first World Series press pin?

11 What is the preferred area between the seams of a baseball for signing autographs?

12 What is the highest grade on the conditioning scale that a sports collectible can receive?

13 What do you call an envelope that includes a postmark with the date and time from the city of a historical sporting event?

14 What do you call a letter that often comes with an autographed item certifying its validity?

15 What year did The Topps Company, Inc. first produce a set of baseball coins?

16 What do you call a world championship ring sold with the initials "(SS)"?

17 What is the most valuable newspaper with a historic sports headline?

18 What do you call a new baseball or football jersey that you buy in a store for the purpose of obtaining a player's autograph?

19 Sports memorabilia referred to as vintage material was produced before what year?

20 How much is a game-used Babe Ruth baseball bat worth?

INDEX

Answers

1. *Lou Gehrig's 1927 New York Yankees jersey*
2. *A facsimile autograph*
3. *Former Cincinnati Bengal's kicker Pat McInally*
4. *The 1929 Yankees were the first to issue jerseys with numbered backs*
5. *Phantom pins*
6. *Babe Ruth, Lou Gehrig, Jackie Robinson, Roberto Clemente*
7. *Joe DiMaggio, May 19, 1949, $500*
8. *Food Issues*
9. *Bill Russell, $600*
10. *1911 Philadelphia A's*
11. *The sweet spot*
12. *Mint*
13. *First day cachet*
14. *Certificate of Authenticity*
15. *1964*
16. *Sales sample*
17. *1919 Chicago Tribune with Shoeless Joe Jackson's confession, $2,500*
18. *A replica jersey*
19. *1970*
20. *$25,000*